Delicious Decisions

COOKING WITH
CALIFORNIA IN MIND

BY THE JUNIOR LEAGUE OF SAN DIEGO

EDITED BY FRANKIE WRIGHT
ILLUSTRATIONS BY JOYCE KITCHELL
DESIGN BY BONNIE SCHWARTZ

Delicious Decisions represents the culmination of three years of tireless effort by members of the Junior League of San Diego. When the project was first conceived, one of the primary goals was that it be an all-league effort. In the true spirit of voluntarism, members fulfilled that goal through their donation of spectacular recipes, hours of testing, imaginative title ideas, marketing efforts, and constant support and enthusiasm.

Bonnie Schwartz, Frankie Wright, and Joyce Kitchell have added a very necessary and impressive professional flair. The extra effort, care, and energy they gave to the project was invaluable.

The Cookbook committees have been unimaginably hardworking and dedicated. Their brainstorming, inspiration, and unwavering confidence have made *Delicious Decisions* a pleasure to produce.

On behalf of the Junior League, we wish to thank Great American First Savings Bank and Nordstrom for their generous donations.

Finally, credit for a great title goes to Susan McClellan.

Kim Jessop
Janis Betts
Cookbook Chairmen 1984-87

Cookbook Committee Members
1984–1987

Chairmen 1984–87
Kim Jessop   *Janis Betts*

Recipe Chairmen
Pam LaMantia   *Jill Limber*

Design Chairmen 1985–86
Nora Newbern   *Kathy Knotts-Lavine*
Jennifer Heft

Testing Chairmen
Libby Levine   *Linda Wilson*

Marilyn Adams	*Karen Luce*
Chris Andrews	*Leslee Jo Machov*
Vickie Barrett	*Dawn Matthiesen*
Kimberly Blair Cheatum	*Lucy Means*
Melinda Cohelan	*Eleanor Navarra*
Nancy Coleman	*Diane Pruett*
Geri Derman	*Mary Rathbun*
Karen Ferm	*Kathee Risser*
Christelle Frost	*Kay Towner Stalle*
Mari Hamlin	*Eleanor Swinehart*
Margaret Anne Lozuk	

Advisors
Joy Frye   *Anne Otterson*

DONORS

Great American First Savings Bank
Nordstrom

For freely giving of their time and expertise,
answering a multitude of questions,
contributing to and supporting the efforts of
The Junior League of San Diego, we also thank . . .

R. Craig Schafer and Cynthia B. Tillinghast
of Advance Marketing Services
Catamaran Resort Hotel
Payne Johnson
Art Jacobs
Lou Cummins
Susan Kelly
Helen Hays
Ellen Rolfes
Suzi Spafford
Janine Rees
Yvonne Larsen
Allison Gildred
Karon Luce
Joanne Webb
San Diego Trust and Savings Bank
Mr. and Mrs. Richard Woods
Rickie Sevadjian

The Junior League of San Diego would like to thank its members and their friends who contributed so much to this book.

RECIPE CONTRIBUTORS

Marilyn Masquelier Adams
Mary Adams
Tommi Lane Adelizzi
Adela Agsten
Kathy Alameda
Betty Barwise Alexander
Helen Lee Alexander
Sally M. Allen
Stacy Blair Alley
Alicia Toomey Amberg
Nancy Anderson
Liz Andress
Christine L. Andrews
Suzanne Andrews
Betsy Anthony
Pamela Armbuster
Liz Armstrong
Karen Volz Bachofer
Kathleen Baczynski
Phyllis Hom Bailey
Jane Booth Baker
Susan Barksdale
Victoria Fink Barrett
Alixanne Baxter
Ellen G. Bergman
Janis Betts
Catherine Blair
Betsy Blakely
Callie Goodrich Blasutta
Anne Bleier
Marla Brayshay Blom
Sarah Haugh Boehm
Janet Boyd
Charleen Cirese Boyl
Carol Brewer
Gini Brooks
Mrs. Dorothy Brown
Hilary H. Broyles
Susan Brubaker
Diana Bryggman
Mrs. Phillip A. Burgess
Mrs. Rosalind B. Burkhart
John M. Burnham
Kim Burst
Roberta M. Campbell
Vicki J. Carlson
Mrs. James H. Carmel
Gloria Carroll
Mrs. Stanley Carroll
Mrs. William R. Carson
Sandra G. Carter
Margaret Kelly Cavallin
Ginger Champ
Constance E. Charles
Kimberly Cheatum
Ginger Christison
Dana Ayers Christl
Loyce R. Clark
Suzanne Bryan Coates
Joanne R. Collins
Pam Conner
Azile Cooper
Kathy Cordero
Emily Corleto
Cynthia Ann Cotter
Mrs. Brad Couture
Marlou Crabtree
Susan Cramer
Elizabeth Davidson
Sue Davidson
Bernice Davin
Irene Davis

Louise Davis
Jodie Deal
Geri L. Derman
Laurie Dermody
Katy Dessent
Ann C. Dixon
Jane Doe
Cynthia Douglas
Virginia W. Dunn
Debbie Dutton
Cindy Dreischmeyer
Kay M. Edelmann
Ellen Ehlers
Carolyn Elledge
Janie Emerson
Judith Emery
Lea Erikson
Linda Erlandson
Susan Evanco
Janet Fall
Ann O'Donnell Farias
Penny Faucett
Karen Ferm
Nancy Field
Lila Fillmore
Patricia P. Fink
Mrs. Sheldon R. Fisher
Martha Fortson
Kristen W. France
Judi Freeman
Christelle Frost
Jeanne Frost
G.T. Frost
G.T. Frost, Jr.
Fred Frye
Joy Frye
Mrs. Alvan T. Fuller
Margaret Gaffney
Ann L. Gallagher
Kippy Gambill
Nancy Garrett
Maxine Garrigues
Kristianne Gates
Hilary Gauntt
Mrs. Chester Gavin, Jr.
Mrs. Randall F. Geddes
Torie Geisler
Suzy Gere
Suzanne Gillick-Pew
Fran Gillis
Jean Gillow
Nancy Gilmore
Frances Golden
Sis Goodrich
Kimberly Gotch
Alyson Goudy
Diane R. Grace
Dede Grant
Michael Grant
Hayley Gravette
Kimberly Gravette
Patty Gravette
Mrs. R. Clemson Griggs
Kathy Grimes
Bunnie Guilbert
Sharon Gwinn
Judy C. Haines
Susan L. Halenza
Donna E. Hall
Julie Halliday
Ruth Hamilton
Betty Hamlin

Marisa Hamlin
Virginia Hammond
'Charlie' Haney
Anne Hanna
Betty Hardison
Barbara Harpe
Cathie Hays
Jennifer Little Heft
Karen Emberton Henry
Kiki Henry
Amelia H. Herrmann
Ann Hill
Dorothy Hill
Mrs. Kenneth E. Hill
Betsy Hillyer
Carol Hinrichs
Lynn Hoaglin
Susan Hoehn
Judy Holmes
Kathryn Holtkamp
Cindy Hom
Christy Honkanen
Mrs. John O. Hopkins
Linda Horrell
Pat Horvath
Carmen B. Howe
Susan Theurkauf Howe
Linda Hubbard
Mrs. Michael Huff
Carol Hughes
Gloria Hum
Frances Hunter
Mrs. C. Daniel Ingebrand
Mrs. Richard W. Jackson
Sara F. Jackson
Becky James
Dee Jerge
Jim Jessop
Kim Jessop
Jackie Johnson
Mary Johnson
Mrs. Burton I. Jones
Dominique Kabaker
Jan Ann Kahler
Kathleen J. Kane-Murrell
Molly Karlsgodt
Jean Baumgartner Kauth
Robin Kellogg
Carol A. Kerley
Lisa Kiacz
Lori J. Kimball
Florence King
Mary King
Maureen Pecht King
Gingi Kinninger
Lisa Botte Kleist
Lisa Klinker
Windie Key Knoth
Kathleen Knotts-Lavine
Sigrid Koebel
Linda Koravos
Annie Krause
Karen Kritzer
Karen M. Ladner
Mr. & Mrs. Thomas R.
   Ladner
Sally La Dow
Mrs. David C. Lake
James LaMantia
Pamela F. LaMantia
Yvonne Larsen
Sandy Lavoy

RECIPE CONTRIBUTORS

Mrs. J. Mark Lawson
Ana Lyon
Wendy Ledford
Allyson Ledsam
Veronica Lee
Mary Lehr
Margery Le Laurin
Beth Leshan
Laura Levine
Libby Levine
Nancy Levy
Patti Ligon
Elizabeth Limber
Jill Limber
Joan Lovell
Margaret Anne Lozuk
Karen Johnson Luce
Dorothy Lyles
Mrs. Edward S. Lynds, Jr.
Darcy W. Lynn
Lorna 'Lori' Lynn
Leslee Jo Machov
Caroline MacKenzie
Kathleen Major
Janet Mance
Debbie Malloy
Betsy Manchester
Anne Marasco
Jane D. Marsh
(In Memory of) –
   Nancy H. Martin
Fran Marxen
Joyce Mason
Carole Coutts Mayo
Catherine McCarthy-Payne
Susan Nash McClellan
Betsy McClendon
Pam McCullough
Mrs. Alan J. McCutcheon, Jr.
Lynn McFadden
Chris McGregor
Susan McKean
M. Hope Meek
Connie Melhorn
Neita Menke
Ruthann Mercer
Anne Messmer
B.A. Mierlot
Connie Burke Miller
Kimberly Miller
Pat Miller
Mickey Mitchell
Martha M. Moffett
Linda Moore
Luanne P. Moore
Carol L. Morley
Isabel M. Morris
Wendy Morris
Carol A. Morrison
Jill Morton
Mary Bryant Mosher
Priscilla L. Moxley
Mrs. William R. Moylan
Pat Mudge
Noreen Mulliken
Mary Jane Murphy
Bettye S. Myers
Eleanor Scott Navarra
Ann Nelson
Nora Hom Newbern
Linda Nickel
Melanie Nickel

Julie Cowan Novak
Karyl Tomb O'Brien
Anna Frances O'Dea
Mrs. Nina O'Hern
Suzanne Guilbert Ohlfest
Aggie Olson
Anne Otterson
Candace Overlie
Sabra G. Packard
Eve Page
Patsy Iverson Page
Peggy Palmer
Vicky Strohl Parish
Dr. Haddon Peck
Ray Peet
Peggy Pehler
Mary Pelkey
Patti Peltz
Gloria Peters
Mrs. Paul W. Petersen
Laurie O. Petter
Mrs. Thomas J. Pike
Kay Pinkham
Meredith M. Pollak
Elizabeth Ponder
Sandra Abernethy Poole
Jill Q. Porter
Julie G. Porter
Missy Post
Carolyn Prosi
Diane Pruett
Suzanne Quayle
Deborah L. Quillin
Nancy C. Ramsayer
Mary McIntyre Rathbun
Harriet Mench Reade
Laurie Reck
Tom Reck
Belle Colochis Reed
Patricia Reeder
Judy Rees
Susan Regan
Bonnie Reid
Carolyn Rentto
Vivian Rich
Marty Atwell Richard
Carre Brown Ridgway
Maria Ring
Nancy Ringewald
Kathee Petersen Risser
Mariam Robbins
Holly Robinson
Ruth W. Robinson
Mariann B. Robson
Charles Rockcastle
Victoria Rodriguez
Charlotte Rowe
Betsy Eager Rudee
Lea Rudee
Joan G. Rusnak
Susan Ryan
Patti Sanborn
Alice Saunders
Marla Scheffler
Sandra L. Scherling
Diane Gaffney Schmidt
Jerri Schmidt
Marcia Schofield
Clem Schwartz
Sandy Schweibert
Vivian B. Serafin
Rickie Sevadjian

Mrs. Edward T. Shadek
Dode Shaw
Ellinor Shinner
Mrs. A. Kelley Shooter
Barbara Shooter
Martha Shumaker
Peggy Bruen Siegener
Barbara Snell
Trudy N. Snell
Phyllis Snyder
Saren L. Spicer
Brooke Squires
Kay Towner Stalle
Mrs. Harold B. Starkey
Linda Starkey
Mrs. Guy Stone
Nancy Stork
Erin Stout
Missy Stucky
Kathy Stumm
Mary Talbot
Jeannie Terry
Betsy Thomas
Susan Thomas
Tina Thomas
Anne N. Thompson
June N. Thompson
Lynne Thompson
Susan W. Thompson
Jill Thorton
Kathryn Townsend
Joanne Tucker
Georgia Tzaferos
Anne Stephens Vafis
Sheila Vardaman
Irene Vaughn
Ann R. Verhoye
Lisa Hamlin Vieira
Dorothy Vought
Kay Vroman
Renne V. Walter
Sally Walter
Mary Ellen Walther
Marilee Warfield
Peggy Watson
Peggy Anne Watson
Katherine Welch
Jill Henn West
Peggy Wheatcroft
Kathryn A. Whistler
Jan White
R. Shelton White
Bam Whitebrook
Marie C. Widman
Jennifer Wilson
Linda Wilson
Marilyn Wilson
Mrs. Pete Wilson
Susan Wilson
Diana Wirtz
Betty Wohlford
Tricia Craven Worley
Priscilla Wright
Gayle Yeakle
Carol Yorston
Gayle Hom Zemen
Peggy Zimmerman
Sally Ann Zoll
Maxine Zuest

RECIPE TESTERS

Marilyn Adams
Melanie Alexander
Alicia Amberg
Marjo Andersen
Liz Andress
Christine Andrews
Suzy Andrews
K. C. Armour
Carol Arnett
Mary Baker
Susan Barksdale
Vickie Barrett
Quaintance Bartlett
Alixanne Baxter
Myra Beare
Marla Bendrick
Janis Betts
Anne Bleier
Sheila Bobenhouse
Sarah Boehm
Christy Bookwalter
Charleen Boyl
Chris Brannen
Amy Bremicker
Maryellen Bridge
Valerie Bridge
Julie Brooke
Carolyn Pecka Brooks
Hilary Broyles
Mary Gwen Brummitt
Diana Bryggman
Elizabeth Campbell
Robbi Campbell
Vicki Carlson
Gloria Carroll
Sue Charlton
Kimberly Cheatum
Tillie Cheyney
Loyce Clark
Joyce Coates
Carole Cochran
Melinda Cohelan
Nancy Coleman
Patricia Conaty
Pam Conner
Kathy Couture
Marlou S. Crabtree
Konnie Dadmun
Jan Darcy
Linda Davis
Louise Davis
Geri Derman
Laurie Dermody
Linda Dieckmann
Penelope Dudek
Debbie Dutton
Lea Erickson
Karen Ferm
Diane Feuerstein
Ellen Fife
Lila Fillmore
Kim Fisher
Terri Fleming
Martha Fortson
Judi Freeman
Christelle Frost
Joy Frye
Nancy Gabel
Maxine Garrigues
Hilary Gauntt
Suzy Gere
Karen Gilligan
Patty Gravette
Kathy Grimes

Carol Guess
Sharon Gwinn
Susan Halenza
Julie Halliday
Ruth Hamilton
Mari Hamlin
Pam Hartley
Jennifer Heft
Margie Heft
Laurel Helmers
Eileen Hennessey
Janice Hinds
Susan Hoehn
Judy Holmes
Christy Honkanen
Martha Houshar
Rebecca Howe
Susan Howe
Gail Hubbard
Marie Huff
Carol Hughes
Gingie Hunstad
Ellie Jacobs
Melissa Jeffers
Kris Jeffery
Dee Jerge
Jerry Jessop
Kim Jessop
Galen Justice-Black
Jan Ann Kahler
Kathy Kane-Murrell
Molly Karlsgodt
Jean Kee
Elizabeth Kelley
Carol Kerley
Windie Knoth
Kathleen Knotts-Lavine
Perry Kurtz
Karen Ladner
Pamela LaMantia
Nancy Lambron
Sandy LaVoy
Wendy Ledford
Beth Leshan
Libby Levine
Nancy Levy
Jill Limber
Margaret Anne Lozuk
Karen Luce
Dorothy Lyles
Lorri Lynn
Ana Lyon
Leslee Machov
Janet Mance
Anne Marasco
Brenda J. Martin
Dawn Matthiesen
Karen Mayo
Kathy McCarthy
Catherine McCarthy-Payne
Debbie McCray
Chris McGregor
Lucy Means
Jane Meyers
Kimberly Miller
Pat Miller
Barbara Mora
Wendy Morris
Noreen Mulliken
Eleanor Navarra
Nora Newbern
Julie Novak
Karey O'Patry

Suzanne Ohlfest
Susan Oliver
Pam Palisoul
Vicky Parish
Diane Pastore
Sandra Pay
Mercedes Pederson
Carol Penniman
Mary Peshel
Melody Petersen
Laurie Petter
Suzanne Pew
Sallie Poet
Julie Porter
Christine Prindle
Carolyn Prosi
Ann Pyle
Eileen Quigley
Mary McIntyre Rathbun
Trish Reeder
Janine Rees
Judy M. Rees
Diane Remick
Robin Renert
Vivian Rich
Marty Atwell Richard
Lisa Richards
Maria Ring
Nancy Ringewald
Kathee Risser
Holly Robinson
Elise Streicher Rogerson
Audrey Rohde
Elizabeth Roy
Betsy Rudee
Susan Ryan
Alice Saunders
Marla Scheffler
Sandy Scherling
Diane Schmidt
Rickie Sevadjian
Jill Shrader
Martha Shumaker
Anne Silliman
Sheryl Singer
Rita Solberg
Laurie Spiegler
Kristina Starkey-McCarty
Susan Stone
Marg Suesse
Julie Sullivan
Mary Talbot
Tina Thomas
Lynne Thompson
Kay Towner Stalle
Diane Tregurtha
Joanne Tucker
Mary Van de Camp
Vickie Venne
Ann Verhoye
Lisa Vieira
Cathy Walsh
M. E. Walther
Susie Warren
Vail Warren
Peggy Watson
Peggy Anne Watson
Nancy Wiener
Linda Wilson
Susan Wilson
Deb Wood
Tricia Craven Worley
Marcia Younie

Contents

Introduction   XI

Imaginative Approaches
APPETIZERS   1

Warm Welcomes
BREADS AND BRUNCHES   41

Fresh Sensations
SOUPS AND SALADS   81

Marvelous Complements
VEGETABLES, RICE, PASTA   153

Sumptuous Abundance
SEAFOOD, POULTRY, MEATS   193

Sweet Finishes
DESSERTS   265

Index   303

Imaginative Approaches

FRESH ASPARAGUS WITH SESAME DIP

2 pounds young asparagus
¾ cup oil
2 tablespoons sesame seeds
1 large egg
2 tablespoons white wine
  vinegar
1 teaspoon honey
1 clove garlic, minced
1 tablespoon soy sauce
Salt, to taste

Asparagus can be prepared in advance and refrigerated. Snap tough ends off asparagus and peel any mature stalks. In a large frying pan, bring about one inch of water to a boil. Add enough asparagus to cover bottom of pan and simmer uncovered until barely tender when pierced, about three to four minutes. Drain and immerse immediately in cold water. Repeat until all asparagus is cooked. Drain and refrigerate.

To prepare dip, heat ¼ cup oil in saucepan over medium-low heat and stir in sesame seeds. Cook until seeds are golden, about three to five minutes. Add remaining oil and remove from heat. Allow to cool. Whisk together egg, vinegar, and honey. Slowly blend in a thin stream of the oil mixture. Blend in soy sauce and garlic. Add salt. (Use a blender or food processor, if desired.) Refrigerate, allowing flavors to blend.

This recipe doubles easily and can also be served as a "salad," simply by using the sesame dip as a dressing for the chilled asparagus.

YIELD: 6 SERVINGS

Asparagus grows best in cool, foggy environments, and tastes best when newly picked from a spring crop. Peak season is from March through May. Quality asparagus is firm with compact tips no wider than the stalks. Stems should be white only on the ends and the entire green portion should be smooth, shiny, and tender. Thin, young shoots are the most delicious and uncooked, have a nutty flavor.

STUFFED CHERRY TOMATOES

This recipe doubles easily and works well as a basis for creative additions or substitutions.

2 pounds bacon
½ cup finely chopped
** scallions**
½ cup mayonnaise
24 firm cherry tomatoes
1 bunch Italian parsley

Good cherry tomatoes are firm but yielding to the touch and fragrant. They should also be thin-skinned and, for best flavor, locally grown. Unless they are completely ripe, store them at room temperature; otherwise refrigerate.

Cook bacon until crisp, drain on paper towels, and break into small pieces. In a bowl, mix bacon, scallions, and mayonnaise. (Fresh homemade mayonnaise results in a better tasting appetizer. See our recipe on page 134.)

Wash and dry tomatoes and remove stem from each. Place each tomato stem side down and use a sharp serrated knife to cut off the round bottoms. Remove pulp with a spoon or melon scoop. Invert tomatoes on paper towels or rack for 30 minutes to drain.

Fill each tomato with the bacon mixture. Refrigerate several hours or overnight. Before serving, rinse and drain parsley and remove stems. Garnish each tomato with a leaf of parsley and spread remaining parsley on a serving platter. Arrange tomatoes on parsley, or a bed of shredded lettuce, which will keep them from rolling.

YIELD: 24 APPETIZERS

CALIFORNIA CAVIAR

3 ounces sour cream
8 ounces cream cheese,
  softened
1 tablespoon lemon juice
1½ teaspoons grated onion

3 tablespoons chopped
  cilantro
Freshly ground black
  pepper, to taste
2 ounces black caviar

Mix sour cream with cream cheese until very smooth. Fold in lemon juice, onion, cilantro, and ground pepper until well blended. Transfer to a serving dish. Gently fold in the caviar. Refrigerate at least two hours before serving. Garnish with a dab of caviar and cilantro leaves.

Serve as a spread for unsalted crackers or water biscuits.

YIELD: 8 TO 10 SERVINGS

Presentation is essential to appetizers that appeal, and presentations can range from elegantly decorated platters to a simple garnish. In this recipe, we set aside a few cilantro leaves and extra caviar to arrange on top of the spread. Not only does this "announce" the ingredients, it adds that important visual touch—the one that catches the eye, then the appetite.

CHEESE SQUARES

These appetizers taste good hot or cold. Prepare a day ahead and reheat in oven or microwave.

⅔ of a single crust pie
  pastry
3 cups heavy cream
4 egg yolks
2 whole eggs
5 cups grated Cheddar
  cheese

4 tablespoons flour
Salt, to taste
Dash Tabasco
1½ tablespoons dried
  minced onion
1 teaspoon dry mustard

Preheat oven to 375 degrees. Grease a 13 x 9 glass baking dish. Prepare the pie pastry and line bottom of dish. Bake about 10 minutes. Remove from oven to cool.

Blend together all remaining ingredients. Pour onto pastry and bake 30 to 40 minutes. Allow to cool slightly before slicing into squares.

YIELD: 48 SMALL SQUARES

A substitution for heavy cream is ¾ cup milk with ⅓ cup butter added.

CAVIAR SOUFFLE ROLL

¼ cup flour
1 cup milk
3 egg yolks
Ground nutmeg, to taste
Pinch of salt
5 egg whites

Filling:

12 ounces cream cheese
2 tablespoons cream
1 tablespoon lime juice
2 tablespoons caviar

Caviar is delicate and requires gentle handling when being cooked or added to other ingredients. Otherwise, it can easily turn to mush. As a general rule, caviar should be the last addition to a recipe.

Preheat oven to 350 degrees. Line a cookie sheet with aluminum foil and pinch up foil around edges. Butter and flour well.

In a small saucepan, blend flour with ¼ cup milk until all lumps dissolve. Add remaining milk and stir over heat until mixture thickens. Remove from heat and allow to cool. In a small bowl, beat egg yolks. Whisk flour mixture vigorously and gradually add egg yolks. Whisk in nutmeg and salt. Set aside.

Beat egg whites and fold into egg yolk mixture. Pour onto prepared cookie sheet and bake 15 to 20 minutes. When souffle has browned, remove from oven and cover with damp tea towel. Invert the pan and separate souffle from foil. Roll up in tea towel and set aside to cool.

Combine cream cheese, cream, and lime juice until well blended. Unwrap souffle and spread with cheese mixture. Spread caviar on top. Roll up. Chill and slice to serve.

YIELD: APPROXIMATELY 16 APPETIZERS

GRECIAN FLAMING CHEESE

This appetizer is tangy and delicious. Jerry G. Bishop, owner of the Greek Islands Cafe at San Diego's Seaport Village, recommends serving it hot along with Greek olives, peppers, and perhaps a cold beer—and adds, "Kaleorexi!" That's Greek for a favorite California expression, "Enjoy!" This recipe is for one cheese square, but you may wish to make several. They should be made one at a time or in separate skillets.

**Kefloteri or Kefalotere (a
    hard, goat's milk cheese),
    about ½ to ¾ inch thick
¼ cup olive oil
1 egg, beaten
¼ cup flour, approximate
1 jigger Ouzo or Metaxa
    (or other brandy or
    cognac)
½ lemon**

Cut cheese into a six-inch square. Wrap in foil or plastic and chill thoroughly. Heat oil in a small cast iron skillet (or heavy Teflon-coated pan). Dip cheese in egg and coat with flour on both sides. Fry in very hot oil, turning once, until golden brown, but do not overcook or cheese will melt and stick to pan. Pour on brandy, ignite it, then douse the flame by squeezing all the juice from the lemon half on the flame and over the cheese.

Slide cheese from pan onto a warm serving plate. Pour pan juices over cheese. Cut cheese into bitesize pieces. Place at least five toothpicks into each piece. Serve with crusty bread for sopping up juices and with lemon wedges for adding extra tang.

YIELD: 4 SERVINGS

CREAMED CAMEMBERT CHEESE

Serve this as a spread for crusty bread or crackers. For an attractive presentation, add slices of fresh fruit to the serving platter. Note that the marinating time for the cheese requires advance preparation.

10 ounces ripe Camembert cheese
¾ cup dry white wine
½ cup fresh bread crumbs
5 tablespoons unsalted butter, softened
Brandy, salt, cayenne, to taste
1 cup California blonde pistachios, shelled and unsalted

Camembert is a soft, cow's milk cheese with a cream-colored center and white, moldy crust. Like Brie, this cheese deteriorates rapidly after it has reached its peak of ripeness. Overripe, it smells of ammonia. The cheese is ripened from the outside by a mold that transforms texture and taste from a hard and chalky blandness to the rich cheese so coveted. California can lay claim to some excellent soft cheeses, particularly the Rouge & Noir Camembert produced in Petaluma.

To flavor the cheese, remove rind and cut into large pieces. Place pieces in nonmetal bowl. Pour wine over cheese and marinate for at least twelve hours or overnight.

Toast bread crumbs in a 350-degree oven for about two minutes. Set aside. Drain the wine-soaked cheese on paper towels. (Do not discard marinade.) Pat tops and sides to dry. Mash together cheese and butter, adding some of the wine marinade as you work. Cheese can be flavored at this point with brandy, salt, or cayenne.

Line a small, round mold with foil or waxed paper. Press half of the cheese mixture into the mold and top with half of the pistachios. Add the rest of the cheese and smooth the top with a spatula. Cover and chill mixture until firm, about three hours.

Chop the remaining nuts and spread them on waxed paper. Spread half the bread crumbs on the bottom of a serving platter. Unmold and unwrap the cheese. Roll the edges in the nuts. Place the cheese on top of the bread crumbs on the platter. Pat the remaining crumbs on top.

YIELD: 4 TO 6 SERVINGS

CURRIED CHICKEN BALLS

This recipe can be doubled or tripled easily and is ideal for advance preparation.

4 ounces cream cheese
2 tablespoons mayonnaise
1 cup cooked chopped
chicken
1 cup sliced blanched
almonds
2 teaspoons curry powder
1 tablespoon finely
chopped chutney
½ teaspoon salt
½ cup flaked coconut
Seedless grapes, seedless
raisins, apple (optional)

Bring cream cheese to room temperature and combine with mayonnaise in a mixing bowl. Blend until smooth. Add chicken and almonds (chopped, if slices are large). Add curry, chutney, and salt. Mix well. Shape into small balls and roll in coconut. Refrigerate before serving.

For presentation, place balls in the center of a round serving platter, ring with washed seedless grapes off stems, and surround grapes with seedless raisins. Core and slice a tart apple (Granny Smith or Jonathan) into even slices. With a knife, square off the edge of each slice. Dip slices in lemon juice and place slices, peel side up, evenly spaced between raisins at opposite sides of the platter.

YIELD: APPETIZERS FOR 4 TO 6 PEOPLE

CARPACCIO

2 pounds lean top round
  steak
6 tablespoons wine vinegar
4 shallots, finely chopped
½ cup chopped parsley
½ cup drained capers
1 teaspoon lemon zest
1 cup olive oil
3 teaspoons coarse salt
3 teaspoons freshly ground
  pepper
2 cloves garlic, chopped

One lemon rind will grate to one tablespoon. Lemon zest, or any citrus zest, should include only the colored part of the peel, which contains the aromatic oils. The white pith is very bitter.

Steak must be fresh and sliced very thin, no more than a sixteenth-inch thick. Freeze meat partially before slicing or have your butcher prepare it. Be sure meat is completely trimmed of sinews and fat. Place slices between two sheets of waxed paper and pound until paper thin. Cut slices into wide strips and arrange on a serving platter.

Brush vinegar over meat and lift edges so all meat is covered. Sprinkle on shallots, parsley, capers, and lemon zest. Mix together oil, salt, pepper, and garlic. Drizzle over meat and allow meat to tenderize in this marinade at least 30 minutes.

As a finger food, carpaccio can be drippy. Serve with thin slices of crusty French bread.

YIELD: APPROXIMATELY 24 APPETIZERS

MUSTARD CHICKEN ON CUCUMBER ROUNDS

2 chicken breasts, boned
  and skinned
1 tablespoon Dijon mustard
1 clove garlic, minced
2 tablespoons unsalted
  butter, melted
⅓ cup chopped fresh
  parsley
¾ cup freshly grated
  Parmesan cheese
2 seedless English
  cucumbers
Fresh rosemary,
  finely chopped

Slice chicken into strips. Mix together mustard, garlic, butter, parsley, and ½ cup cheese. Toss chicken pieces in sauce and marinate three to four hours at room temperature.

Preheat oven to 350 degrees. Pour chicken and sauce into a baking pan and bake 40 minutes or until chicken is tender and cooked through. Remove from oven to cool. Puree chicken in a blender or food processor, adding sauce as needed to achieve a chunky paste consistency. Refrigerate until chilled.

Cut each cucumber crosswise into quarter-inch slices. Top each slice with a spoonful of chicken puree. Sprinkle with remaining cheese and top with rosemary.

YIELD: APPROXIMATELY 30 APPETIZERS

Cucumbers. We've seen jugglers toss them. We've seen slices on sun-bathers eyelids. And we even know a cat named Cucumber, who is decidedly cool. These green wonders have been included in the diets of many cultures since ancient times. The long ones, usually wrapped in plastic, are seedless. The small ones, Kirbies, are delicious pickled or not. And the large waxed ones are the most common and often peeled before eaten. Jugglers rinse off the wax with hot water.

CURRIED CHICKEN ON RADICCHIO LEAVES

2 chicken breasts, boned
  and skinned
4 tablespoons unsalted
  butter
½ cup honey
¼ cup Dijon mustard
1 tablespoon salt
1 tablespoon curry powder
¼ cup chopped toasted
  almonds

1 large head radicchio
Flat-leaf parsley (garnish)

Preheat oven to 375 degrees. Lightly butter a baking pan
(9 x 13 inches).

Use a sharp knife to slice chicken into bitesize strips.
Melt butter in a saucepan, add remaining ingredients
except almonds, and stir until well blended. Stir in
chicken, covering all pieces. Pour chicken and sauce into
baking pan and bake uncovered 30 minutes or until
chicken is tender and cooked through. Remove from oven
to cool. Stir in almonds and refrigerate.

Rinse and crisp radicchio. Tear leaves in half and spoon
curried chicken on each leaf. Garnish with sprigs of parsley.

YIELD: 8 TO 10 SERVINGS

PORK SATAY

¾ pound boneless pork
  shoulder
¼ cup freshly squeezed
  lemon juice
2 tablespoons soy sauce
2 cloves garlic, chopped
¾ teaspoon sugar
½ teaspoon salt

Sauce:

2 tablespoons peanut butter
1 tablespoon butter
1 tablespoon soy sauce
1 teaspoon lemon juice
½ teaspoon crushed red
  pepper
½ teaspoon sugar
¼ cup heavy cream

Trim off all fat and cut pork into one-inch cubes. Mix lemon juice, soy sauce, garlic, sugar, and salt and whisk until well blended. Marinate pork in this mixture at least three hours, or overnight in the refrigerator.

Preheat oven to 425 degrees. Mix sauce ingredients in saucepan. Cook over medium heat and stir until sauce thickens. Place pork cubes in a baking dish, cover with sauce, and bake for 15 to 20 minutes.

Serve hot on small skewers, with two cubes per skewer.

YIELD: APPROXIMATELY 12 APPETIZERS

MARINATED PORK SKEWERS

3½ pounds lean boneless
  pork, cubed
½ cup minced onion
⅓ cup peanut oil
⅓ cup freshly squeezed
  lemon juice
¼ cup soy sauce
3 tablespoons dark rum
1½ tablespoons sugar
1½ tablespoons fresh
  ginger, peeled and
  minced
3 small cloves garlic,
  minced
Red pepper flakes, to taste

Ginger root is available all year. Spicy hot and yet sweetly aromatic, ginger is versatile—excellent for baked sweets and for flavoring savory dishes. The Asians who have settled in California and influenced cooking styles have popularized the use of ginger root. Look for roots with few knobs and un-shriveled skins. Wrap loosely and refrigerate, or peel and store covered with sherry in a sealed container. The root can also be frozen whole and sliced as needed.

Place pork in a shallow pan. Mix together remaining ingredients, pour over pork, and toss to cover all pieces. Marinate covered in the refrigerator at least six hours or overnight.

Arrange cubes on skewers and grill over hot coals about 15 minutes, basting occasionally and turning once. Pork should be cooked through, but tender. Remove cubes from skewers, pierce with toothpicks (two cubes per pick), and place on a serving platter with slices of fresh fruit.

YIELD: APPROXIMATELY 50 APPETIZERS

CRAB STUFFED MUSHROOMS

Steve Hargraves of El Crab Catcher in La Jolla sends this delicious and popular offering. The stuffing makes about three cups. Depending on the size of mushrooms, the number of mushrooms you need will vary. Any leftover stuffing can be refrigerated for later use.

2 pounds large mushrooms,
  stems removed
2 ounces Jack cheese,
  shredded

Stuffing:

1 cup fresh Dungeness
  crabmeat, cooked and
  flaked
5 ounces Jack cheese,
  shredded
1 cup fresh sourdough
  bread crumbs, toasted
½ cup unsalted butter
1 egg, beaten
1 bunch scallions and tops,
  minced
½ sweet red pepper,
  chopped
1 cup dry white wine
½ teaspoon oregano
1 tablespoon snipped fresh
  dill
Salt and freshly ground
  pepper, to taste

Preheat oven to 350 degrees. Wipe mushrooms with a soft cloth until clean. Combine all stuffing ingredients, mixing thoroughly. Stuff each mushroom cap, and top each with a small mound of Jack cheese. Bake 15 minutes.

SHRIMP AND CRAB MOUSSE

1 envelope unflavored
  gelatin
⅓ cup cold water
10 ounces pureed tomatoes
8 ounces cream cheese
1 cup mayonnaise
¾ cup finely grated onion
¾ cup finely chopped
  celery
Dash salt
Dash Tabasco
½ teaspoon lemon juice
1½ cups cooked, chopped
  crab and shrimp

Soften the gelatin in the cold water. Bring tomatoes to a boil, reduce heat, and slowly whisk in gelatin-water mixture. Add cream cheese and stir until melted. Remove from heat and cool to room temperature. Whisk in mayonnaise, onion, celery, salt, Tabasco, and lemon juice. Stir to blend completely. Refrigerate for about 15 minutes, then fold in crab and shrimp. Transfer mixture to a serving bowl or decorative mold and refrigerate overnight. (A fish mold is ideal for this mousse. For decoration, use olives for the eyes, fresh parsley or fresh dillweed for eyebrows, sliced almonds for scales, and pimiento strips on the tailfin.)

Serve with crackers, cocktail toasts, or with slices of dark rye or pumpernickel.

YIELD: APPROXIMATELY 12 SERVINGS

TOASTED BREAD CRISPS

½ pound unsalted butter
1 teaspoon chopped fresh
  savory
1 teaspoon chopped fresh
  basil
4 tablespoons chives
1 loaf thin-sliced white
  bread

Preheat oven to 350 degrees. Soften the butter without melting it. Add herbs and chives to butter and mix well.

Remove crusts from bread. Use a rolling pin to flatten slices. Spread butter-herb mixture on one side of each slice. Roll the slices on the diagonal, beginning with a corner, with the herb spread on the inside. Place on a lightly buttered cookie sheet and bake uncovered for about 35 minutes.

These bread crisps are delicious right out of the oven, but they keep well if prepared ahead. Once removed from the oven, allow them to cool completely before wrapping in foil to store. Any leftovers can be chopped and used as croutons.

Substitute fresh herbs for the dried varieties whenever possible. Use one to two tablespoons of fresh for each teaspoon of dried, or more if desired. When using dried herbs, rub the amount between your palms before adding to the recipe. This releases aromatic oils and enhances flavor. The intensity of dried herbs, which tends to diminish with age, can vary; add dried herbs to taste.

CRAB PUFFS

8 ounces cream cheese,
   softened
1 teaspoon lemon juice
¼ teaspoon white pepper
½ teaspoon salt
6 ounces fresh crabmeat,
   cooked and flaked
¼ cup finely chopped
   scallions
½ cup shredded lettuce
¼ cup minced water
   chestnuts
1 pound won ton wrappers
1 egg, beaten
6 cups peanut oil

Scallions, or green onions, are baby onions with a mild flavor. Some varieties tend to be sweeter and milder than others, and can be used almost extravagantly in salads. Others with more bite are better for cooking. Both the bulbs and green tops carry the flavor, but both are highly perishable. Peak season is from May through July.

To prepare filling, combine cream cheese, lemon juice, pepper, and salt until well blended. Fold in crabmeat, scallions, and water chestnuts. Chill for two hours.

Spoon filling in the center of each won ton wrapper. Moisten edges with egg and fold into triangles. (If won ton wrappers are purchased frozen, allow package to thaw in its original wrapper at least two days in the refrigerator.)

Preheat oil in a deep fryer for about 20 to 30 minutes. Fry puffs about two to three minutes until golden brown. Drain on paper towels. Serve warm with a variety of hot mustards, wasabi, or horseradish dip.

YIELD: 60 APPETIZERS

ONION RINGS

6 large Bermuda or Spanish
   onions
1 cup evaporated milk
1½ cups water
2 eggs, beaten
½ teaspoon salt
1½ cups self-rising flour
¼ teaspoon paprika
¼ teaspoon freshly ground
   pepper
Dash cayenne (optional)
Peanut oil for frying

Peel and slice onions in half-inch slices and separate into rings. Refrigerate in a bowl of water until ready to use.

Combine milk, water, eggs, and salt. Chill. Sift together flour and seasonings. Heat peanut oil (about 1½ inches deep) to about 375 degrees in a skillet, or use a deep fryer. Dip onion rings into milk mixture, then fluff in flour mixture. Repeat. Fry a few at a time in the oil until golden brown. Remove and drain on paper towels.

Keep fried rings warm in a 200-degree oven while working. Serve immediately.

YIELD: 5 TO 6 SERVINGS

If onions like such a dry environment, why do they make us cry? Moisture causes onions to decay quickly, so store them in a cool, dry, well-ventilated place. And keep them in the dark. Not that they deserve it for sending their eye-irritating volatile oils into the air when sliced, but because they need the dark to stay fresh.

SALSA

Salsa is an e
egg dishes, o

5 ripe tomat
7 ounces gre
   chopped
½ onion, fine
2 cloves garli
½ bunch cila
¼ cup red w
¼ cup freshl
   lemon juic
1 teaspoon o
1 teaspoon sa

Drop tomato
remove, dous
in a food pre
remaining in;
until well mi
bowl. Proces:
salsa, strain j
meatier porti

Chill at least
refrigerated o

YIELD: 10

*Fresh green chilies—
jalapenos, serranos, or
poblanos—are becoming
easier to find. If a recipe
calls for fresh chilies, the
canned versions are not a
good substitute. The reverse
is more favorable. Char fresh
chilies to enhance their
flavor, peel the skins, and
remove seeds and veins. If
the chilies are too hot or
spicy for a recipe, soak them
in salted water for about an
hour. Chop and add as a
substitute for canned chilies,
but take care with the
amount added.*

*Blue-veined cheeses are
produced in many countries;
the French Roquefort is
probably the best known.
Two other cheeses should be
considered when blue (or
bleu) cheese is called for:
Gorgonzola, from Italy, is
crumbly when aged and ex-
cellent for dressings and
sauces because of its exceptional melting qualities. (A
young Gorgonzola is creamy
and sweeter, ideal for
spreads.) Stilton, the English
version that sends some folks
into raptures, is semifirm
and has a mellow cheddar
flavor.*

WALNUT ROQUEFORT TARTINES

⅓ cup unsalted butter,
   room temperature
6 ounces Roquefort cheese
1 tablespoon cognac
   or armagnac
4 ounces walnuts, coarsely
   chopped
1 loaf *pain de mie* or
   coarse-grain country
   bread
Radishes, celery, pears,
   thinly sliced (garnish)

Whip butter lightly to a smooth paste. Add cheese and
blend. Add cognac, mixing well. Fold in walnuts and
distribute evenly. (If a food processor or blender is used,
chop walnuts first, process butter and cheese, taking care
not to over process, and complete the recipe by hand in a
separate bowl.)

Slice bread into small squares or triangles and toast. Bread
will be crispier if prepared a day in advance. Allow toasted
pieces to cool completely, wrap, and store in a dry place.

Preheat oven to 350 degrees. Spread small amount of
Roquefort butter to edges of bread slices. Place on racks on
a cookie sheet and heat in oven until butter has melted
and saturated bread. Remove from oven and garnish each
slice with radishes, celery, or pear slices.

YIELD: 8 TO 10 SERVINGS

CEVICHE

The fish for this recipe must "cook" in the
least twelve hours or longer.

1 pound fresh white fish
   (red snapper, white sea
   bass, sole)
Juice of 3 lemons
1 cup ice water
½ cup vegetable juice
2 tablespoons green chili
   salsa
1 large firm tomato, diced
6 green onions, diced
¼ medium bell pepper,
   diced

½ cup chop
1 large car
12 stuffed
   sliced
1 tablespoo
1 clove gar
½ cup cho
½ cup cho
Salt, to tast

Remove bones and cut fish into quarter-inc
in a glass or ceramic bowl and cover with
Gently toss fish to coat pieces completely.
marinate until it is no longer transparent, h
in the citric acid. Toss fish in juice occasio
results. Marinated fish can be prepared a d
desired. Drain off lemon juice and rinse fis
water.

Combine remaining ingredients and mix wi
Marinate at least two hours before serving.
warm tortilla chips.

YIELD: 6 TO 8 SERVINGS

SHRIMP DIP

For the most flavorful results, this dip should be prepared
at least eight hours before serving.

¾ pound shrimp
8 ounces cream cheese
¾ cup mayonnaise
½ cup chopped celery
½ cup chopped scallions
1 tablespoon lemon juice
1 tablespoon fresh dill,
   snipped
½ teaspoon horseradish
Dash of garlic salt
Dill sprigs (garnish)

Cook shrimp until done in boiling water, drain, and douse
immediately in cold water. Peel and devein. Refrigerate four
of the shrimp for garnish and chop or process the remaining shrimp into small pieces.

Blend cream cheese and mayonnaise together until light
and smooth. Add remaining ingredients and mix well.
Drain all water from chopped shrimp. Fold shrimp into
cream cheese mixture until evenly distributed. Transfer dip
to a serving dish and refrigerate for at least eight hours or
overnight.

Before serving, arrange four whole shrimp in center of dip
in a swirl (heads in center, tails fanning out in the same
direction) and place dill sprigs between shrimp. Serve with
a variety of crackers.

YIELD: APPROXIMATELY 3 CUPS

GUACAMOLE WITH HOMEMADE SALSA

The extra salsa this recipe makes can be stored up to two weeks in a covered glass container in the refrigerator. Salsa is an essential ingredient for many Mexican dishes, but it also spices up hamburgers, cold meats, and vegetable soups, just to name a few.

Salsa:

2 fresh green chilies, seeded and chopped
6 yellow chilies, seeded and chopped
2 ripe tomatoes, seeded and chopped
10 ounces stewed tomatoes
6 tablespoons corn oil
8 cloves garlic, minced
1 teaspoon dried oregano
3 teaspoons chopped fresh cilantro
Salt and freshly ground pepper, to taste

Guacamole:

4 ripe avocados, peeled and chopped
½ cup salsa, or more to taste
1 ripe tomato, seeded and chopped
1 scallion with top, finely chopped
Cilantro sprigs (garnish)

Avocados do not ripen on the tree and are rarely found ripe in markets. Buy them two or three days in advance, but do not store them in the refrigerator—they'll turn dark and lose flavor. When ripe, the fruit will be tender to the touch at the stalk base. When sliced open, a ripe avocado will have the consistency of firm butter.

Combine salsa ingredients, using care when handling chili peppers. (Wear rubber gloves to avoid skin irritation; remove seeds under cold running water; avoid getting any juice in eyes.)

Combine avocados, salsa, tomato, and scallion in a large bowl. Store covered in refrigerator until ready to serve. To serve, stir guacamole, transfer to a serving dish, and garnish with cilantro sprigs.

YIELD: 6 TO 8 SERVINGS

VERSATILE MUSTARD SAUCE

¾ cup dry mustard
1 cup white wine vinegar
1 cup brown sugar
2 beaten eggs

Combine mustard and vinegar in a glass jar, shake well, and refrigerate overnight. Add brown sugar and beaten eggs. Cook in a double boiler over medium heat, stirring constantly for 20 minutes.

While the sauce is warm, pour it over a brick of cream cheese to serve as a spread for unsalted crackers or water biscuits. Or serve it over pieces of smoked chicken or turkey skewered with cooked bacon and small slices of fresh pineapple, apple, or sweet red pepper. This sauce can also be served cold with smoked salmon or gravlax on thin bread slices with sprigs of fresh dill for garnish.

YIELD: APPROXIMATELY 3 CUPS

CURRY DIP

½ cup sour cream
¼ cup mayonnaise
½ teaspoon curry powder
Cayenne, to taste
1 tablespoon catsup
¼ teaspoon Worcestershire
  sauce
1 clove garlic, minced
¼ teaspoon horseradish
Fresh cilantro or celery
  leaves (garnish)

Combine all ingredients and mix until well blended. Refrigerate at least six hours or overnight, allowing flavors to blend.

Stir before serving and garnish with chopped cilantro or celery leaves. Serve with cold, crisp vegetables that have been chopped or sliced into bitesize pieces. Or serve on toasted pita bread triangles.

YIELD: APPROXIMATELY 1 CUP

BAKED SHRIMP IN WINE AND BASIL SAUCE

With the tails of these shrimp curled over the side of a baking dish, this appetizer is an eye-catcher. The shrimp can't carry all the delicious sauce however. Serve a loaf of warm, sliced sourdough for dipping.

1 cup melted butter
¼ cup dry white wine
¼ cup minced parsley
2 tablespoons freshly
  squeezed lemon juice
3 large cloves garlic,
  minced
4 tablespoons chopped
  fresh basil
1 teaspoon Worcestershire
  sauce
1 teaspoon Tabasco
½ teaspoon salt
2 pounds shrimp, shelled,
  deveined, tails intact
½ cup dry, unseasoned
  bread crumbs

Preheat oven to 450 degrees. Combine the first nine ingredients in a bowl and mix well. Remove a fourth of this mixture and set aside.

In a shallow baking dish (or small quiche dishes), pour in part of the sauce. Place the shrimp around the rim (or rims) with tails over the side, being sure the meat is well coated. Mix the bread crumbs with the remaining sauce and sprinkle over the dish. Bake 10 to 15 minutes. Serve warm with slices of sourdough.

YIELD: APPROXIMATELY 10 SERVINGS

VEGETABLES WITH AIOLI SAUCE

Although associated with antipasto platters, aioli sauce is just too versatile to be limited. Here, it's a dip for colorful vegetables, but it can also be used as a spread for hot roast beef or steak sandwiches. Aioli sauce improves if flavors are allowed to blend several hours or overnight.

1 large sweet red pepper
1 large yellow pepper
2 medium heads fennel
16 cooked artichoke petals
1 pound snow peas,
  blanched and chilled

Sauce:

2 egg yolks, room
  temperature
8 cloves garlic, minced
Salt and freshly ground
  pepper, to taste
Juice of 1 lemon
1 teaspoon Dijon mustard
1½ cups olive oil
1 green pepper, hollowed
  (to hold sauce)
Fennel leaves (garnish)

Slice the red pepper into strips and the yellow pepper into wheels, removing all seeds and veins. Slice the fennel into strips. Arrange these with the artichoke petals and snow peas on a serving platter.

Whisk egg yolks until light and frothy. In a blender or food processor, add yolks and garlic and blend. Combine salt, pepper, lemon juice, and mustard and add to garlic mixture. With motor running, add oil slowly in a steady stream until mixture is thick and shiny. (This may occur before all oil is added.) Chill sauce for several hours or overnight. Serve in the shell of a pepper with all veins and seeds removed. Garnish sauce with fennel leaves.

YIELD: 8 SERVINGS

Sweet peppers, cousins to tomatoes and potatoes, are generally bell-shaped and have a lovely green color. (Tapered peppers, a paler green, possess more flavor.) When allowed to ripen completely on the vine, green peppers sweeten and turn red. The red, yellow, and purple bell peppers are gaining popularity, though more expensive, because of their taste and visual impact.

CALIFORNIA FAJITAS

This requires advance preparation for both the marinated meat and salsa. Extra salsa can be stored in the refrigerator up to two weeks.

3 pounds flank steak
½ cup freshly squeezed
   lime juice
⅓ cup olive oil
⅓ cup tequila
4 cloves garlic, minced
1¼ teaspoons dried
   oregano
¾ teaspoon ground cumin
½ teaspoon ground cloves

1 dozen flour tortillas
Grated Jack cheese
Chopped scallions and tops
Chopped cilantro

Salsa:

2 fresh green chili peppers,
   seeded and chopped
6 white or yellow chili
   peppers, seeded and
   chopped
2 large ripe tomatoes,
   chopped
10 ounces stewed tomatoes
6 tablespoons corn oil
8 cloves garlic, minced
1 teaspoon oregano
2 teaspoons chopped fresh
   cilantro
Salt and freshly ground
   pepper, to taste

Slice meat across the grain into thin strips. Combine lime juice, oil, tequila, garlic, and spices. Pour over meat to cover all pieces. Marinate four to eight hours at room temperature, tossing occasionally.

Combine salsa ingredients in a quart container. Cover and refrigerate at least eight hours.

Grill meat over hot coals until medium rare. Slice flour tortillas in half, wrap and warm in oven until soft. Place strips of meat into each tortilla, top with salsa, cheese, onions, and cilantro. Roll each fajita, warm in the oven (if desired), and arrange on a serving platter.

YIELD: 48 APPETIZERS AND 1 QUART SALSA

ROLLED TACOS WITH CRABMEAT

These tacos are served "cool" and are delicious for warm weather get-togethers.

1 ripe avocado, mashed
2 tablespoons freshly
  squeezed lime juice
1 clove garlic, minced
6 flour tortillas
1 head romaine lettuce,
  shredded
1½ cups shredded Jack
  cheese
1 pound cooked crabmeat,
  chilled
2 tomatoes, chopped
½ cup sliced pitted olives
Hot taco sauce

Blend avocado with lime juice and garlic. Set aside. Slice tortillas in half and fill each with lettuce, cheese, crabmeat, tomatoes, and olives. Spoon on taco sauce to taste. Roll each as tightly as possible and arrange on a serving platter. Top with blended avocado.

YIELD: 12 APPETIZERS

CRANBERRY CHUTNEY

Chutney is a much overlooked appetizer idea. Use it for canapes, as a filling for miniature muffins, or serve it over a cream cheese spread on water biscuits. It is delicious with thinly sliced smoked ham or chicken.

1 pound fresh cranberries
2 cups sugar
1 cup water
1 cup freshly squeezed
   orange juice
1 cup raisins, coarsely
   chopped
1 cup chopped walnuts
1 cup chopped celery
1 cup finely chopped tart
   apples (Granny Smith)
1 tablespoon grated orange
   peel
1 teaspoon ground ginger
3 tablespoons finely
   chopped candied ginger

Cranberries are gaining popularity in California cooking. Too long ignored, these berries have a high acid content that gives them their bright, tart flavor and a longer storage life than other berries and many fruits. Cranberries are easily frozen without damage, but should be sorted first. Plump, shiny berries are best.

Prepare some sterile storage jars. Sort through and discard bruised cranberries. Rinse thoroughly, drain, and combine with sugar and water in a large saucepan. Place over medium heat and bring to a boil, stirring occasionally. Simmer for 15 minutes and remove from heat. Stir in remaining ingredients.

When completely cool, pour chutney into jars and refrigerate. This recipe works well if prepared at least two hours before serving, but better if allowed to refrigerate a week or more. It will keep up to three weeks if refrigerated.

YIELD: APPROXIMATELY 7 CUPS

Warm Welcomes

BREADS AND BRUNCHES

Homemade bread lusciously spread with homemade flavored butter is a treat to be shared, perfect for a brunch that glows with delicious aromas and good company. When we think of brunch, we imagine bright blue skies, sunlight streaming through colorful bouquets, fresh air, fresh fruit, and a glorious table setting of sweet coffeecakes, tea breads, jams, jellies, and fluffy egg dishes rich with herbs from the garden. The good life. Good food.

The breads in this section are excellent brunch additions, although some are certainly appropriate anytime; others, with a sorbet or heaped with ripe berries, would be wonderful desserts. Our pancakes and muffins make us a little nostalgic, remembering those occasional Sunday night suppers that were more like breakfast. We loved that simple surprise as kids, and our kids love it, too.

Pancakes can be downhome or the height of epicurianism; a delicious decision either way. Decisive cooks will find many such options here. From Mexican Corn Spoon Bread to Pflaumenkuchen, a delectable plum tart, and from Mushrooms Benedict to the rich Crustless Crab Quiche, the recipes offer approaches that suit casual gatherings or fulfill that tantalizing brunch fantasy we conjure whenever brunch and sunny California mornings come to mind.

MEXICAN CORN SPOON BREAD

Corn is one of the foundations of Mexican cooking. Though usually ground, corn is sometimes called for fresh, and the sweet, white variety is preferred. (For this recipe, substitute a 17-ounce can of cream-style corn if fresh corn is not available.)

4 ears fresh white corn
Cream
½ pound unsalted butter
¾ cup sugar
4 eggs
4 ounces Ortega chilies,
  diced
¼ teaspoon salt
½ cup grated Jack cheese
½ cup grated Cheddar
  cheese
1 cup flour
1 cup yellow corn meal
4 teaspoons baking powder

Before baking breads or muffins, have all ingredients at room temperature unless the recipe specifies otherwise. Naturally, this requires some prior planning, and for those of us whose passion for baking tends to be impulsive, it's a lesson in patience.

Preheat oven to 300 degrees. Butter a 9 x 14 inch baking pan. Remove husks and silk from corn. Draw a very sharp knife through each row of kernels. Slice corn off the cobs, and over a bowl, scrape the cobs to remove all pulp and milk. Add enough cream to make about 2¼ cups and cook slowly over medium heat until kernels are tender, stirring often. Do not boil. Remove from heat to cool.

Cream butter and sugar. Add eggs one at a time, mixing well after each. Add chilies and blend into egg mixture. Add corn, salt, and cheese and mix well. In a separate bowl, sift flour, corn meal, and baking powder together. Combine with the corn mixture. Bake uncovered for one hour. Slice when cooled slightly.

YIELD: 8 TO 10 SERVINGS

FRENCH BREAD

Greet your guests with that unmistakable aroma of fresh
bread baking in the oven.

2½ cups warm water
1 teaspoon sugar
2 envelopes yeast
7 cups unbleached flour
1 tablespoon salt
1 tablespoon vegetable or
  olive oil

The dough for this bread must be refrigerated at least two
hours before baking. It can be prepared a day in advance
and refrigerated overnight. When ready to bake, preheat
oven to 375 degrees. Grease two cookie sheets or four
baguette pans.

Warm a large mixing bowl with hot water. Heat 2½ cups
water to a temperature in the range of 105 to 115 degrees.
In the warm bowl, dissolve the sugar and yeast in the
water. When the mixture proofs (foams), stir in the flour,
salt, and oil until the dough is very stiff (or mix with a
dough hook on low speed). Knead the dough for about 10
minutes until no longer sticky, then cover with a damp
towel and let it rest for 20 minutes in a warm place.
Punch down and shape into two large loaves on cookie
sheets or place in smaller baguette pans. Cover with plastic
wrap and refrigerate.

Remove from refrigerator 30 minutes before baking. Bake
for 35 to 40 minutes until well browned. The loaves are
done if they sound hollow when lightly rapped.

YIELD: 2 LARGE LOAVES OR 4 SMALL LOAVES

*Yeast is a relatively slow
leavening agent. It produces
carbon dioxide that causes
dough to rise, but it also
possesses a characteristic
flavor much loved. Baking
powder is faster acting and
better for "weak" doughs,
such as those for quick
breads. The powder is a
blend of acid and alkali
(nearly always baking soda).
Double acting powder pro-
duces a first set of carbon
dioxide bubbles when added
to the batter, creating air
pockets. When heated (baked),
more bubbles are formed and
the trapped gas creates
pressure and steam that
expands the batter even
more.*

HOT CORNSTICKS

Laurel and Paddy Rainwater provide this recipe from their restaurant menu. Rainwater's on Kettner is located in downtown San Diego, close to the harbor's sparkling lights.

1 cup flour
3 tablespoons sugar
2 teaspoons baking powder
¾ teaspoon salt
1 cup yellow corn meal
1 egg, well beaten
10 ounces creamed corn
¾ cup milk
2 tablespoons shortening

Look for bread flour if you plan to do much baking. This flour is produced to closely resemble professional bakers' flour and results in breads with high quality texture and flavor.

Preheat oven to 425 degrees. Preheat cast iron cornstick pans in oven until very hot.

Combine flour, sugar, baking powder, and salt. Add corn meal and mix thoroughly. In a separate bowl, combine egg, corn, milk, and shortening. Add to dry ingredients and stir until just mixed.

Butter hot cornstick pans and fill each slot about two-thirds full with batter. Bake until golden brown, about 20 minutes.

YIELD: 18 CORNSTICKS

LEMON TEA BREAD

This bread can be served warm or at room temperature. Its sweetness is counteracted slightly by a rich lemon flavor, a taste that combines well with sliced pears or a raspberry sorbet. To freeze, wrap in foil when the bread has completely cooled.

½ cup unsalted butter
1 cup sugar
2 eggs
Rind of 1½ lemons, finely
  grated
1½ cups flour
1½ teaspoons baking
  powder
½ teaspoon salt
½ cup milk

Glaze:

¼ cup powdered sugar
Juice of 1½ lemons

Preheat oven to 350 degrees. Grease and flour bread pan (8½ x 4½ x 3 inches).

Cream butter and add sugar gradually, working until light and fluffy. Add eggs one at a time and beat until light. Add lemon rind. In a separate bowl, combine dry ingredients and add to the sugar-butter mixture alternately with milk, ending with flour. Beat on low speed only until mixtures are combined.

Pour batter into loaf pan and bake one hour or until a wooden pick inserted in the center is withdrawn clean. Remove bread from oven and prepare glaze by mixing powdered sugar and lemon juice until smooth. Pour over bread while it is still hot in the pan. Allow glazed bread to cool at least 15 minutes before removing from pan.

YIELD: 1 LOAF OR 8 LARGE SLICES

One medium lemon yields two to three tablespoons of juice. To get the most juice from a lemon (or lime or orange), have it at room temperature or warm it under hot water, then break down the pulp by rolling it on a hard surface.

STRAWBERRY NUT BREAD

A delicious accompaniment to fresh fruit, this bread can be served cold with a dollop of whipped cream topped with lemon zest, or served lightly toasted with a spread of cream cheese or one of the flavored butters on page 62.

3 cups sifted flour
1 teaspoon baking soda
1 tablespoon cinnamon
2 cups sugar
3 eggs, beaten
1½ teaspoons vanilla
   extract
1 cup corn or safflower oil
Grated rind of 1 lemon
3 cups chopped
   strawberries
¾ cup chopped pecans

Remove caps from strawberries only after washing. Wash the berries just before you plan to use them. The caps protect the flavor and texture of the fruit. Strawberries store best as one layer. Remove from deep flats and place cap-side down on a plate and store covered in the refrigerator. Use as soon as possible; strawberries ripen no further once picked.

Preheat oven to 350 degrees. Grease and flour two loaf pans (9 x 5 x 3 inches).

In a large bowl, combine flour and baking soda until soda is well distributed. Add cinnamon and sugar. Mix well. In a separate bowl, combine eggs, vanilla, oil, and lemon rind. Spoon in strawberries and gently blend to cover with the liquid. Add this mixture in batches to the dry ingredients and incorporate by hand. Fold in nuts.

Pour batter into loaf pans and bake one hour or until a wooden pick inserted in the center comes out clean. Allow loaves to cool in the pan for five minutes, then turn out onto wire cooling racks. Do not slice until ready to serve.

YIELD: 2 LOAVES

SWEET POTATO MUFFINS

½ cup butter
1¼ cups sugar
2 eggs
1¼ cups cooked sweet
  potatoes, mashed
1½ cups flour
2 teaspoons baking powder
¼ teaspoon salt
1 teaspoon cinnamon
¼ teaspoon nutmeg
1 cup milk
¼ cup pecans, chopped
½ cup raisins, chopped

Preheat oven to 400 degrees. Grease 1½-inch muffin tins.

Cream butter and sugar. Add eggs and mix well. Blend in sweet potatoes. In a separate bowl, sift flour with baking powder, salt, cinnamon, and nutmeg, and add to sugar-butter mixture alternately with milk. Do not overmix. Fold in nuts and raisins. Fill muffin tins two-thirds full. Bake 25 minutes.

These muffins freeze well and are an excellent accompaniment to ham or turkey dinners. For brunch or afternoon tea, they can be cut in half and filled with whipped butter or cream cheese and a light spread of blackberry jam, for example. Or serve with pear or apple wedges and slices of Stilton cheese.

YIELD: 24 MUFFINS

Sweet potatoes are at their peak in November and December. They are not yams, which are of a different plant variety, and they generally have a sweeter, nuttier flavor. Choose firm sweet potatoes with dark peels for the best flavor.

Before chopping raisins or dates, butter the blade of your knife or sprinkle the fruit with oil to coat. Either will keep them from sticking. To plump raisins for bread or muffin recipes, pour boiling water over them to cover, let stand for a minute or two, then drain and dry on paper towels.

APPLESAUCE MUFFINS

The batter for these muffins can be prepared up to two days ahead if refrigerated in an airtight container.

1 cup applesauce,
  unsweetened
1 cup dark brown sugar
3 tablespoons molasses
½ cup unsalted butter
1¾ cups flour
1 teaspoon baking soda
½ teaspoon salt
1½ teaspoons cinnamon
½ teaspoon cloves

Molasses are derived from the refined sugar of sugar cane sap. Light molasses are used as table syrup. Dark molasses (blackstrap) have a stronger flavor that gives baked goods a rich, hearty taste.

Preheat oven to 375 degrees. Butter 12 small muffin tins.

Mix applesauce, brown sugar, molasses, and butter until well blended. In a separate bowl, sift together flour, baking soda, salt, cinnamon, and cloves. Make a well in the center and add applesauce mixture. Gently fold in by hand until dry ingredients are moist.

Spoon batter into muffin tins and bake 25 to 30 minutes or until muffins are browned and an inserted wooden pick is withdrawn clean. Take tins from oven and allow to cool slightly before removing muffins. Cool on racks.

YIELD: 12 SMALL MUFFINS

SOUR CREAM AND CINNAMON COFFEECAKE

1 cup unsalted butter
2 cups sugar
2 eggs
1 teaspoon vanilla extract
2 cups flour
1½ teaspoons baking
   powder
1 cup sour cream
¾ cup chopped pecans
3 tablespoons cinnamon
4 tablespoons brown sugar
3 tablespoons sugar

Preheat oven to 350 degrees. Grease and flour a bundt pan.

Cream butter, sugar, eggs, and vanilla. In a separate bowl, sift together flour and baking powder. Add to creamed mixture. Fold in sour cream. Pour half of the mixture into pan.

Mix together remaining ingredients and sprinkle half on top of the batter in the pan. Repeat the layers and swirl the batter with a knife. Bake approximately 50 minutes to one hour. Remove pan from oven and allow to cool before removing cake.

YIELD: 16 SERVINGS

Ground cinnamon can be adulterated and of inferior quality to cinnamon sticks. Sticks contain more of the essential oil that gives the bark its aroma and sweet, hot flavor.

APPLE-NUT COFFEECAKE

Small, golden delicious apples are suggested for this cake.

2 cups sugar
1 cup unsalted butter
2 eggs
2 cups flour
2 teaspoons baking soda
2 teaspoons cinnamon
½ teaspoon salt
1 cup chopped pecans
4 small apples

To keep nuts and fruit from settling to the bottom of bread dough during baking, fluff them in flour before adding to the batter.

Preheat oven to 350 degrees. Grease and flour a baking pan (12 x 8 inches).

Cream together sugar and butter until fluffy. Add eggs one at a time and mix well. In a separate bowl, sift together flour, soda, cinnamon, and salt. Add to creamed mixture and fold in by hand until all ingredients are combined. Fold in chopped nuts.

Peel and dice apples and incorporate into batter. Pour batter into pan and bake one hour or until inserted wooden pick comes out clean. Allow to cool before removing from pan.

YIELD: 12 SERVINGS

PFLAUMENKUCHEN

This plum tart is "very rich, very simple, and very elegant" according to Maureen Clancy, Food Editor for the *San Diego Union*. The recipe comes from her mother-in-law and uses Pflaumen, Italian prune plums, which are available in August and September.

Pastry:

2 cups flour
1 teaspoon baking powder
Pinch salt
14 tablespoons unsalted
 butter, cold
1 egg yolk, slightly beaten
⅓ cup sugar

Tart:

25 to 30 Pflaumen
3 to 4 tablespoons sugar
2 tablespoons unsalted
 butter
Whipped cream (topping)

In a food processor, place flour, baking powder, salt, and butter (broken into small pieces). Process in quick pulses only until mixture has the consistency of oatmeal flakes. Add egg yolk and sugar and process until well blended. Do not overprocess. Chill for several hours or overnight.

Preheat oven to 350 degrees. Remove pastry from refrigerator and roll out *quickly*. Line a 10-inch tart pan, preferably one with fluted edges and a removable bottom. Bake for about 15 minutes or until dough just starts to turn golden. Remove from oven.

Cut plums into quarters, remove pits, but do not peel. Arrange plums on the pastry in concentric circles that slightly overlap. Sprinkle with sugar and dot with butter. Bake about 30 minutes or until plums are softened and the crust is well browned. Serve warm or at room temperature and top with freshly whipped cream.

YIELD: APPROXIMATELY 4 TO 6 SERVINGS

Plums, juicy sweet, come in colors as rich as their taste: scarlet, blue, to a purple so deep it's nearly black. A good, ripe plum is a plum. And, of course, a good plum is sometimes hard to find. Seek out locally grown varieties in season and you'll know what "plum good" is all about.

FROSTED OATCAKE

Delicious is an understatement for this coffeecake.

2 cups oat flakes
2½ cups boiling water
1 cup unsalted butter
1½ cups sugar
2 cups brown sugar,
    packed
4 eggs
2 teaspoons vanilla extract
3 cups flour
2 teaspoons baking soda
1 teaspoon salt
1½ teaspoons cinnamon
½ teaspoon nutmeg

Frosting:

½ cup unsalted butter,
    melted
1 cup brown sugar
⅓ cup cream
1 cup chopped walnuts
    (or pecans)
1½ cups flaked coconut

Nutmeg is an aromatic seed, and its red, weblike husk is the spice mace. Both seed and husk are dried before use.

Preheat oven to 350 degrees. Grease a rectangular baking pan (9 x 13 inches). Add oat flakes to boiling water. Reduce heat and cook until water is absorbed. Remove from heat and set aside.

In a large mixing bowl, cream butter and gradually beat in sugars. Blend in eggs and vanilla and beat for two minutes. Add the oat mixture. Mix the dry ingredients in a separate bowl. Gradually add to the sugar-butter mixture and blend in. Mix for two minutes.

Pour batter in pan and bake 30 minutes or until a wooden pick inserted in the center comes out clean. Allow cake to cool before removing from pan.

Combine the frosting ingredients and spread over the cooled cake.

YIELD: 8 TO 12 SERVINGS

OATCAKE WITH CARAMEL NUT TOPPING

This coffeecake is very moist and has the advantage of being delicious hot from the oven.

1¼ cups boiling water
1 cup quick rolled oats
½ cup unsalted butter
1½ cups sifted flour
¾ cup sugar
1 teaspoon baking soda
½ teaspoon salt
¾ cup brown sugar
3 eggs, beaten

Topping:

1 cup unsalted butter
½ cup half and half
1 cup brown sugar
1 cup chopped pecans
1 tablespoon grated
  lemon rind

Preheat oven to 350 degrees. Butter and flour a baking pan (9 x 13 inches).

In a prewarmed mixing bowl, pour boiling water over oats, add butter, and stir until well combined. In a large bowl, sift together flour, sugar, baking soda, and salt. Stir in brown sugar, eggs, and oat mixture. Beat at low speed until combined. Pour into pan and bake 35 to 40 minutes or until inserted tester is withdrawn clean.

Prepare topping as cake bakes. Combine butter, half and half, and brown sugar in a saucepan. Cook, stirring constantly, until mixture boils. Reduce heat. Simmer, stirring frequently, until slightly thickened, about five minutes. Stir in nuts and grated rind. Spread topping over hot cake. Broil four to five inches from heat for one to two minutes or until topping is bubbly. Serve warm or cold.

YIELD: 12 TO 15 SERVINGS

DATE CAKES

4 tablespoons butter
1 cup sugar
1 egg
1 teaspoon vanilla extract
1 cup boiling water

1 cup chopped dates
1¼ teaspoons baking soda
¼ teaspoon salt
1½ cups flour
1 cup chopped nuts

Preheat oven to 325 degrees. Place paper muffin cups in muffin tins.

In a large bowl, cream butter and sugar. Add egg and vanilla and mix well. In a separate bowl, pour boiling water over dates and stir well. Stir in baking soda and salt. Add to creamed mixture alternately with flour. Fold in nuts.

Fill muffin tins halfway. Bake 25 minutes or until a wooden pick inserted in the center comes out clean.

YIELD: 12 SMALL MUFFIN-SIZE CAKES

Dates are called "the candy that grows on trees." California is the date growing center of the Western Hemisphere, producing exotic varieties and the more common sun-dried dates. These dates are left on palm trees to mature and become juicy, and if rainfall is high during the growing season, they are especially moist and sweet. Top grade dates can be eaten out of hand, like candy; others are used for cooking and baking.

ONE FOR TWO PANCAKE

Dust this pancake with powdered sugar and top with thin lemon slices, or serve with melted butter, honey, and fresh berries.

3 eggs
½ cup flour
¼ teaspoon salt

½ cup milk
2 tablespoons butter, melted

Preheat oven to 450 degrees. Butter a 10-inch ovenproof skillet.

Beat eggs with a fork and slowly add flour, whisking constantly. Stir in salt, milk, and butter. Pour entire batter into cold skillet and bake for 18 minutes. Reduce oven temperature to 350 degrees and bake an additional 10 minutes. Turn pancake onto a plate and serve hot.

YIELD: 2 SERVINGS

FLAVORED BUTTERS

These tasty spreads are ideal for tea breads, muffins, and pancakes.

Whip ½ cup unsalted butter until fluffy and add one of the following combinations, using a food processor if desired:

Raisin Nut Butter

¼ cup finely chopped
  toasted walnuts
¼ cup finely chopped
  raisins
1 tablespoon freshly
  squeezed orange juice
1 tablespoon sugar
1 teaspoon cinnamon

Sweet Citrus Butter

¼ cup honey
1 tablespoon freshly
  squeezed orange or
  lemon juice
2 teaspoons grated orange
  or lemon rind
2 tablespoons sugar
2 teaspoons cinnamon

Almond Butter

1 cup sifted powdered
  sugar
1 teaspoon almond extract
¼ cup finely chopped
  toasted almonds

Honey Fruit Butter

¼ cup honey
2 tablespoons freshly
  squeezed orange juice
1 small banana or peach,
  well mashed

Sugar and Spice Butter

¼ cup firmly packed brown
  sugar
½ teaspoon cinnamon
½ teaspoon nutmeg

Marmalade Butter

½ cup marmalade (lemon,
  orange, or grapefruit) or
  jam (raspberry, peach,
  apricot, currant, cherry,
  among others)

Unsalted butter, or sweet butter, is preferred for cooking and baking because it allows the cook to adjust seasoning. To some, the delicate taste is preferred overall. Freeze unsalted butter to keep it fresh and from absorbing other flavors during storage.

MEXICAN FRENCH TOAST

This fried toast differs from the standard French variety in that no milk is added to the dipping batter. Mexican vanilla, when used, enhances the richness with its distinct flavor and aroma.

½ cup sugar
1½ teaspoons cinnamon
Corn oil for frying
4 eggs
½ teaspoon vanilla
  (pure Mexican white
  preferred)
4 thick slices good quality
  bread

Vanilla pods are gathered off the "vines" of the climbing vanilla orchid plant. They are picked before ripe, boiled briefly, then cured to develop aroma. Cured pods are dark brown and can be stored at home in sugar to be used in cake, candy, and bread recipes. Californians are well aware of the wonderful Mexican vanilla that has its own distinctive flavor.

Mix sugar and cinnamon and set aside. Pour oil in large frying pan to a one-inch depth and heat to very hot. Beat eggs with vanilla and immerse bread slices in mixture. Fry quickly until completely toasted. Remove from oil, pat with paper towels, and coat with sugar-cinnamon mixture.

Serve with butter and heated syrup.

YIELD: 2 TO 4 SERVINGS

SPINACH QUICHE

1 10-inch uncooked pastry shell
2 tablespoons unsalted butter
¾ cup chopped onions
⅓ cup chopped scallions
¼ cup chopped fresh parsley
1 bunch fresh spinach, cooked and well drained
2 tablespoons flour
Salt, to taste
¼ tablespoon freshly ground black pepper
¼ teaspoon nutmeg
Cayenne pepper, to taste
1 tablespoon Worcestershire sauce
2 eggs beaten
1 cup grated Gruyere cheese
⅓ cup freshly grated Parmesan cheese
1¼ cups milk

Preheat oven to 400 degrees. Prick pastry shell and bake for about 8 minutes. Remove from oven and reduce oven temperature to 350 degrees.

Melt butter in a pan over medium heat and saute onions, scallions, and parsley. Add spinach and cook two minutes. Remove pan from heat. Add flour, salt, pepper, nutmeg, cayenne, and Worcestershire sauce, stirring well. In a bowl, whisk together eggs, cheese and milk. Add spinach mixture and stir to distribute ingredients evenly. Pour into pastry shell and bake 45 minutes to one hour, or until knife inserted into center is withdrawn clean.

YIELD: 6 SERVINGS

Spinach can't be praised enough. And it can't be washed enough. It grows in sandy soils that seem to cling to the growing leaves. Leaves can be crinkled or nearly flat, and when freshest, should be deep green and crisp. Buy spinach in rosettes (still on the main stem) whenever possible—it will stay fresher longer.

SEAFOOD AND BROCCOLI QUICHE

2 tablespoons unsalted butter
½ cup chopped scallions
1 cup mushrooms, sliced
1 cup broccoli florets, chopped
3 beaten eggs
½ cup cream
¾ cup cottage cheese
¼ cup whole milk
½ teaspoon salt
½ teaspoon grated lemon peel

Dash nutmeg
½ pound fresh shrimp, peeled, deveined, and cooked
4 ounces fresh crabmeat, cooked and flaked
1½ cups shredded Swiss cheese
1 tablespoon flour
1 10-inch uncooked pastry shell

Preheat oven to 450 degrees. Melt butter in a pan over medium heat and saute scallions and mushrooms until tender. Remove from heat and set aside. Steam broccoli two minutes. Douse in cold water and set aside to drain.

In a large bowl, stir together eggs, cream, cottage cheese, milk, salt, lemon peel, and nutmeg. Add scallions, mushrooms, and broccoli. Chop shrimp and add to egg mixture along with crabmeat. Combine cheese and flour and add to egg mixture. Stir all ingredients until distributed evenly.

Line unpricked pastry shell with heavy duty aluminum foil and bake five minutes. Remove foil and bake an additional five to seven minutes until shell is lightly browned and nearly done. Reduce oven temperature to 325 degrees. Pour quiche batter into hot pastry shell. If necessary, cover edges to prevent over-browning. Bake 35 to 40 minutes or until knife inserted in the middle is withdrawn clean.

YIELD: 6 SERVINGS

CRUSTLESS CRAB QUICHE

2 tablespoons unsalted
  butter
1 sweet red pepper, seeded
  and finely chopped
¼ cup thinly sliced
  scallions and tops
½ pound mushrooms,
  thinly sliced
4 eggs
1 cup sour cream
1 cup cottage cheese
½ cup freshly grated
  Parmesan cheese
4 tablespoons flour
½ teaspoon marjoram
¼ teaspoon salt
2 drops Tabasco
½ pound crabmeat, cooked
  and flaked
2 cups grated Jack cheese

Preheat oven to 350 degrees. Butter a 10-inch quiche pan
or 9-inch deep dish pie pan.

Melt butter over medium heat in a skillet and saute pepper,
scallions, and mushrooms until just tender. Remove from
heat.

In a blender or food processor, blend eggs, sour cream,
cottage cheese, Parmesan cheese, flour, marjoram, salt, and
Tabasco. Pour into large bowl and stir in sauteed vegetables,
crab, and Jack cheese. Mix well. Pour into quiche pan and
bake 45 minutes or until inserted knife comes out clean.
Quiche should be puffed and golden brown. Let stand five
minutes before cutting.

Garnish each slice with a dollop of sour cream and a
scallion top sliced into a fan or brush.

YIELD: 6 TO 8 SERVINGS

BAKED EGGS AND BACON WITH HERB SAUCE

1 pound bacon
1½ dozen eggs

Herb sauce:

¼ cup butter
¼ cup flour
1 cup milk
1 cup cream
1 pound grated sharp
  Cheddar cheese
½ teaspoon marjoram
2 tablespoons chopped
  fresh basil
½ cup chopped Italian
  parsley
Dash salt
½ clove garlic, minced
Buttered bread crumbs
Italian parsley sprigs
  (garnish)

The perfect hard-cooked egg. Many methods have been put forward to achieve it. We think the best way is never to bring an egg to a full boil; that's why we don't use the term "hard-boiled." (We save that and "half-baked" for other uses.) Cover eggs with cold water in a saucepan. Bring water just to a boil, reduce heat so that bubbles rise slowly to the surface. Simmer 20 minutes.

Fry bacon until very crisp, drain, and break into small pieces. Boil eggs until hard cooked, peel, and slice. Preheat oven to 350 degrees.

To prepare sauce, melt butter in a saucepan over medium heat, stir in flour, and cook until bubbly. Slowly add milk and cream. Add grated cheese, herbs, salt, and garlic. Stir until thickened.

In a buttered baking dish, layer half the eggs, bacon, and sauce. Repeat layers ending with sauce. Top with bread crumbs. Bake 20 to 30 minutes uncovered. Garnish each serving with parsley sprigs.

YIELD: 10 SERVINGS

MUSHROOMS AND DAIRY RICHES

Fresh herbs from the garden would beautifully garnish this brunch dish.

10 tablespoons unsalted
    butter
1 pound fresh mushrooms,
    thinly sliced
1 dozen eggs
Dash salt and freshly
    ground pepper

Sauce:

6 tablespoons unsalted
    butter
6 tablespoons flour
1 pint cream (or half and
    half)

---

4 ounces grated Parmesan
    cheese
4 ounces grated Swiss
    cheese
4 ounces grated Cheddar
    cheese

Melt two tablespoons butter in a large skillet over medium heat. Saute mushrooms until tender. Remove mushrooms to a bowl with a slotted spoon and set aside. Reduce skillet heat to low and add four tablespoons butter. Break eggs into large bowl and whisk thoroughly. Add salt and pepper. Pour eggs into skillet and gently scramble. When eggs are like soft curds, stir in remaining butter (cut into pieces, if hard) and sprinkle with salt and pepper. Set aside.

For sauce, melt butter in a separate saucepan over medium-low heat. Stir in flour. Allow mixture to bubble 30 seconds. Stir in cream and whisk over low heat until mixture thickens. Mix half of this sauce with the mushrooms.

Lightly butter an ovenproof casserole and sprinkle with half the Parmesan. Spread a thin layer of cream sauce and place half the scrambled eggs on top. Place mushroom mixture on top of the eggs. Sprinkle with half the Swiss and Cheddar. Add rest of eggs and top with remaining cream sauce and cheese. Broil six inches from heat until cheese bubbles and eggs are heated through. Slice and serve.

YIELD: 6 TO 8 SERVINGS

The mushroom veil—that membrane between the cap and stem—pulls away from the stem if a mushroom loses moisture. Generally, open veils indicate age and mean a shorter storage life, but flavor is not diminished. Mushrooms that have darkened and turned slimy are beyond use, but those that are firm and white with open veils are fresh enough for cooking.

MUSHROOMS BENEDICT

8 thin slices Canadian
  bacon or ham, precooked
½ cup unsalted butter
½ cup chopped green
  onions, including tops
1½ pounds fresh
  mushrooms, sliced
1 teaspoon paprika
2 cups sour cream
Salt and pepper, to taste
4 whole English muffins

Wrap Canadian bacon or ham in foil and warm in the oven.

Melt butter in a large saucepan and saute onions over medium-low heat until transparent. Reduce heat and add mushrooms, paprika, and sour cream. Stir often until thoroughly heated, but do not boil. Remove from heat and add salt and pepper.

Halve, toast, and butter English muffins. Place bacon or ham slices on muffins and pour mushroom sauce on top. Serve immediately.

YIELD: 4 TO 8 SERVINGS

BROCCOLI SOUFFLE

3 cups fresh broccoli florets
1 small onion, chopped
4 tablespoons unsalted
  butter
3 tablespoons flour
½ cup water
Salt and freshly ground
  pepper, to taste
3 eggs, beaten
2 cups shredded Jack
  cheese
1¼ cups freshly grated
  Parmesan cheese

Preheat oven to 350 degrees. Steam broccoli five minutes. Douse immediately in cold water. Drain and place in the bottom of a buttered souffle dish (two-quart capacity).

Saute onion in butter and cook until tender. Stir in flour and slowly add water. Add salt, pepper, eggs, and cheeses. Mix well. Pour over broccoli in souffle dish and bake 40 minutes.

YIELD: 6 SERVINGS

SPANISH SAUCE

This sauce is ideal for Spanish omelettes or served as a chilled topping for sliced avocados or thin slices of flash-fried flank steak.

2 tablespoons unsalted
  butter
½ pound mushrooms,
  sliced
3 stalks celery, sliced
1½ green peppers, cubed
2 onions, cut in wedges
1 clove garlic, minced
6 ounces tomato paste
3 cups whole tomatoes,
  peeled and cooked
2 teaspoons chili powder
1 teaspoon Worcestershire
  sauce
Dash cayenne

Melt butter in a saucepan and saute mushrooms until tender. Add celery, green pepper, onions, and garlic. Cover pan and simmer 10 minutes. Transfer to a pot and add tomato paste. Cut up whole tomatoes and add to pot along with seasonings. Cover and simmer until vegetables are tender.

Flavor improves if sauce is refrigerated overnight and reheated before serving. This sauce can also be frozen.

YIELD: 10 TO 12 SERVINGS

BLINTZ SOUFFLE

This souffle is a sweetie—wonderfully rich, easy to make, and best of all, it can be prepared ahead.

Filling:

8 ounces cream cheese
2 cups small curd cottage
  cheese
2 egg yolks
1 tablespoon sugar
1 teaspoon vanilla extract

Batter:

½ cup unsalted butter,
  softened
⅓ cup sugar
6 eggs, lightly beaten
1½ cups sour cream
½ cup freshly squeezed
  orange juice
1 cup flour
2 teaspoons baking powder

Preheat oven to 350 degrees. Butter a baking dish
(9 x 13 inches) and set aside.

Blend together filling ingredients until smooth. Set aside.
To prepare batter, mix butter and sugar until fluffy, blend
in eggs, sour cream, and orange juice. In a separate bowl,
combine flour and baking powder, "sifting" together with a
fork. Add to butter mixture and blend well. Pour half of
the batter into baking dish. Spread filling over the top with
a knife; some will settle into the batter. Pour remaining
batter over filling. (At this point, souffle can be refrigerated
several hours or overnight, if desired. Cover until ready to
use. Before baking, remove from refrigerator and allow to
stand until at room temperature.)

Bake uncovered 50 to 60 minutes or until puffed and
golden. Serve immediately with toppings of sour cream,
flavored syrup, or assorted jams.

YIELD: 8 SERVINGS

OVERNIGHT SOUFFLE

This recipe should be prepared a day in advance of baking.

4 tablespoons unsalted butter

1 cup fresh mushrooms, sliced

1 large onion, diced

16 slices white bread, crusts removed

1 pound lean bacon, cooked crisp and crumbled

¾ cup diced celery

2 Anaheim chilies, seeds removed, peeled and diced

1 pound sharp Cheddar cheese, grated

Salt and freshly ground pepper, to taste

2 tablespoons snipped fresh dill

1 large tomato, peeled and thinly sliced

6 eggs, lightly beaten

3 cups cream

1 tablespoon Dijon mustard

Melt butter in a saute pan over medium heat. Cook mushrooms and onions for two minutes or until just slightly tender. Remove with a slotted spoon. Dip eight bread slices into pan to butter one side. Place bread, butter side down, in an oblong casserole (13 x 9 x 2 inches). Layer half of the mushrooms and onions, bacon, celery, and chilies on top of the bread and finish with half of the cheese. Season with salt, pepper, and one tablespoon of dill. Repeat the bread layer and the remaining half of ingredients as above, but add tomato slices before cheese.

Thoroughly mix eggs, cream, and mustard and pour over casserole. Cover with waxed paper and refrigerate overnight.

Before baking, allow casserole to stand at least 30 minutes at room temperature. Preheat oven to 350 degrees. Bake casserole uncovered for 45 minutes or until soufflelike consistency is achieved. Remove from oven and cool five minutes before slicing. Leftovers may be frozen.

YIELD: 8 TO 10 SERVINGS

BREAD BOWL SANDWICH

A good choice for entertaining on the casual side.
The ingredients can be varied with a little imagination,
and once assembled, the bread bowl can be frozen and
baked later.

1 round loaf French bread
¼ cup unsalted butter,
  softened
2 teaspoons Dijon mustard
1 pound round steak,
  ground
1 large onion, chopped
2 cloves garlic, minced
Salt and freshly ground
  pepper, to taste
1½ teaspoons dried basil
1½ teaspoons dried
  oregano
1 cup cooked spinach,
  drained
1 cup Jack cheese, cut into
  small cubes

Preheat oven to 400 degrees. Cut through the top of the
bread loaf, forming a lid about four inches in diameter.
Remove soft bread from lid and from inside loaf, leaving a
shell about one-inch thick. Cut soft bread into half-inch
cubes to make three cups. Set aside. Mix butter and
mustard together and spread over the inside surfaces of
the shell.

In a skillet, cook ground beef until browned over medium-
high heat. Crumble meat as it cooks. Reduce heat and add
onion and garlic, and cook until onion is tender. Drain off
all fat. In a large bowl, add salt, pepper, and herbs to meat
and mix well. Add spinach, bread cubes, and cheese. Mix
until all ingredients are thoroughly combined. Pack this
filling into the bread bowl. Set lid in place and wrap loaf
loosely in foil.

Bake 45 minutes. Remove from oven and allow to cool
slightly. Remove foil, and when cool enough to handle,
slice into wedges. Arrange on a serving platter.

YIELD: 6 SERVINGS

MYSTERY ROLLS

When baked, the filling ingredients blend so well they are hard to identify. But it's no mystery why these rolls have been popular in Southern California for many years—they're easy and delicious.

12 French rolls
Unsalted butter, softened,
 to spread
½ pound Cheddar cheese,
 shredded
¼ pound Jack cheese,
 shredded
2 cups pitted olives,
 drained and chopped
3 to 4 scallions with tops,
 finely chopped
3 green peppers,
 finely chopped
4 hard-cooked eggs,
 finely chopped
4 tablespoons wine vinegar
½ to 1 cup olive oil
Salt and freshly ground
 pepper, to taste

Preheat oven to 350 degrees. Cut tops off rolls and scoop out soft bread from tops and bottoms. Butter the inside of tops. (Leftover bread can be whirled in a processor and frozen for use as bread crumbs in other recipes.)

In a large bowl, mix cheeses, olives, scallions, peppers, eggs, and vinegar. Add oil last, in small portions at a time, until mixture is thoroughly moistened but not soupy. Add salt and pepper, and test for seasoning. Fill each roll generously and replace top. Wrap each in wax paper and twist ends tightly.

Bake 30 minutes. (Paper may smoke some.) Remove from oven and allow to cool 15 minutes before serving. Rolls will hold heat if left wrapped.

For variation, use salad peppers, pepperocini, or chili peppers instead of green peppers. Add two cloves of finely minced garlic. Add tomato sauce and increase the number of rolls and chopped solids. Other cheeses can be substituted as well.

YIELD: 12 ROLLS

SANDWICH NICOISE

Prepare a day ahead for an easy, warm weather brunch.

2 loaves French bread,
  unsliced
8 ripe tomatoes, peeled,
  seeded, diced
4 tablespoons chopped
  scallions with tops
1 cup pitted olives,
  chopped
½ cup chopped parsley
½ cup freshly grated
  Parmesan cheese
1 cup tuna
Dash thyme, or more
  to taste
⅓ cup olive oil
⅓ cup dry white wine
Salt and freshly ground
  pepper, to taste
4 drops Tabasco

Cut ends from loaves and dig out soft centers with a fork, making a hollow tube in each. Chop the bread crumbs, add to remaining ingredients, and mix well until thoroughly combined. Stuff each loaf with the mixture. Wrap in foil and refrigerate at least 24 hours.

To serve, cut each loaf into one-inch slices and arrange on a serving platter.

YIELD: 10 TO 12 SERVINGS

Good Parmesan cheese is hard and pungent, and has a sharp, slightly salty taste. Buy imported Parmesan in small amounts, store it tightly wrapped, and grate it yourself just before serving. Pregrated cheese loses flavor, and the grated brands sold in markets only vaguely resemble the original.

TURKEY AND GRUYERE SAUCE IN ROSEMARY CREPES

Crepes:

1¼ cups unbleached flour, sifted
½ teaspoon salt
4 eggs
¼ cup unsalted butter, melted and cooled
1 cup milk
1 cup cold water
¼ cup finely chopped fresh rosemary (or 2 table-spoons dried)

Filling:

4 tablespoons unsalted butter
¼ cup flour
3 cups milk
2 cups grated Gruyere cheese
1 teaspoon salt
¼ teaspoon pepper
1/8 teaspoon paprika
2 teaspoons sherry
1 to 1½ pounds turkey meat, cooked
2 heads green- or red-leaf lettuce, rinsed and crisped

Brunch is an American invention, meant to be informal, comfortable, and to feature light fare. What could be more appropriate to the light and casual dining style many Californians embrace? Brunch should be cheery with a menu that includes the best of plain and fancy.

To prepare crepes, blend all ingredients at high speed. If using a food processor, process 30 seconds, scrape down sides, and reprocess another 30 seconds. Refrigerate batter one hour. Heat a griddle to medium-high. Pour batter onto griddle in ¼ cup amounts for each crepe and spread the batter to thin. Crepes should be about five inches in diameter. Cook until surface bubbles, turn with a spatula and cook until golden brown, about 30 seconds. Remove and stack.

For filling, melt butter until it "foams" in a saucepan. Sprinkle on flour and stir, cooking two to three minutes. Add milk and stir until sauce is smooth and thick. Do not boil. Stir in cheese, seasonings, and sherry. Remove from heat once cheese has melted. Slice turkey into bitesize pieces and add to sauce, covering all pieces.

To serve, tear lettuce and place a leaf on each crepe with curly edge extending over one side of crepe. Spoon turkey and sauce on top and roll crepe into a funnel shape with lettuce exposed on the open end. Use excess lettuce to garnish a serving platter, and place crepes in an arrangement on top.

YIELD: 25 SERVINGS

Fresh Sensations

CUCUMBER SOUP

Walnut lovers might consider adding a few tablespoons of finely chopped walnuts to this recipe.

4 tablespoons unsalted
   butter
1 chopped onion
1 chopped leek
4 cucumbers, peeled,
   seeded, chopped
½ teaspoon salt
Freshly ground pepper,
   to taste
4 cups chicken broth
2 tablespoons dry white
   wine
½ cup cream
½ cup half and half
½ cup sour cream
1 tablespoon fresh dill,
   snipped
1 tablespoon lemon juice
5 drops Tabasco
Thin cucumber slices and
   fresh, chopped chives
   (garnish)

Melt butter in a saute pan and cook onion, leek, and cucumbers until transparent but not brown. Season with salt and pepper and pour into two-quart saucepan. Add broth and wine, bring to a boil, reduce heat, and simmer for 30 minutes. Remove from heat to cool. Pour mixture, in batches, into a blender or food processor and process until smooth. Add cream, half and half, sour cream, dill, lemon juice, and Tabasco. Mix well and chill.

To serve, pour soup into chilled serving bowls and garnish with cucumber slices and chives.

YIELD: 6 SERVINGS

We like leeks. Their mild flavor is well suited to California's love affair with light cuisine and subtle combinations. Most often associated with soups, leeks can also be boiled, even barbecued, with delicious results. Select leeks that are white and firm at the base with tightly furled leaves and use them within a day or two of purchase. Wash leeks carefully; they tend to hold soil. Cut off tops, remove outer leaves, cut in half lengthwise, and rinse thoroughly.

STRAWBERRY SOUP

Prepare this refreshing soup a day in advance for the best result.

2 pints fresh strawberries
1 cup freshly squeezed
  orange juice
1¼ teaspoons instant
  tapioca
Allspice, to taste
Cinnamon, to taste
½ cup sugar
1 teaspoon grated lemon
  peel
1 tablespoon lemon juice
1 cup buttermilk
2 ripe canteloupes, chilled
Fresh mint sprigs and
  lemon slices (garnish)

Many fruits, and even almonds, are of the rose family. And that includes the strawberry, which when ripe and red, is truly beautiful. For the fraise crazy, strawberries can be dressed with a puree of other ripe berries; sprinkled with kirsch, brandies, port, or many other liqueurs and dessert wines; served in champagne or orange juice and curacao; topped with almonds, candied violets, or grated vanilla bean; lavished with whipped cream; or just eaten from a flat, au naturel.

Wash strawberries, dry on paper towels, and remove stems. Set aside a half dozen strawberries. Puree remaining strawberries in a blender or food processor. Strain into a four-quart saucepan and add orange juice.

In a small bowl, mix tapioca with four tablespoons strawberry puree. Add this mixture to the saucepan along with spices. Heat, stirring constantly, until mixture comes to a boil. Cook one minute or until thickened. Remove from heat and pour into a large bowl. Stir in sugar, lemon peel, lemon juice, and buttermilk and mix well. Set aside to cool. Slice the reserved strawberries and fold into soup. Cover and refrigerate at least eight hours or overnight.

To serve, slice canteloupes in half and remove seedy pulp. Pour soup into cavity and garnish with fresh mint. Top with a very thin lemon slice.

YIELD: 4 SERVINGS

COLD ZUCCHINI SOUP

This recipe doubles easily but should be made in two single batches. If fresh dill is not available, consider adding a dash of nutmeg as a substitute, particularly for an early autumn first course.

4 small zucchini, sliced
1 green pepper, chopped
½ cup finely chopped
  onion
3 cups chicken stock
1 cup sour cream (or plain
  yogurt)
1 tablespoon chopped
  Italian parsley
1 teaspoon fresh dill,
  snipped (or ¼ teaspoon
  dried dill)
1 small zucchini, chopped
Salt and freshly ground
  pepper, to taste
4 sprigs dill (garnish)

Set aside four slices of zucchini for garnish and combine remaining zucchini in a large saucepan with green pepper, onion, and chicken stock. Simmer covered for 20 minutes. Strain vegetables, reserving stock.

In a food processor or blender, combine sour cream, parsley, and dill with the cooked vegetables. Add the stock while the machine is running. Turn off machine and stir in chopped zucchini, salt, and pepper. Chill thoroughly.

To serve, pour soup into chilled serving bowls and garnish with zucchini slices and dill sprigs.

YIELD: 4 SERVINGS

In many instances, we've called for Italian flat-leaf parsley in our recipes. Gaining deserved popularity, this parsley is generally available and is better for cooking than the curly parsley so often used. The flavor is subtle and refined, and its appearance is more attractive for garnishes.

ZUCCHINI SOUP WITH THYME

Not many women hold the title of Chevalier du Etats Unis Taste du Vins. Helen Muzzy does, and holds our attention as well with this classic approach to fine cuisine: simple preparation of the freshest ingredients.

4 cups chicken stock
2 tablespoons fresh thyme
  (1 teaspoon dried)
4 cups fresh zucchini,
  unpeeled and diced
1½ cups white onions,
  diced
1½ cups celery,
  finely diced
1 cup unsalted butter
Salt and freshly ground
  white pepper, to taste
Sherry

Heat stock to simmer, add thyme, zucchini, onions, and celery. Cook until liquid is slightly reduced and vegetables are tender. Blend soup in batches with butter added to each batch, leaving about one cup of stock in the pot. Return blended creamy mixture to the pot, salt and pepper to taste, and simmer five minutes. Pour into heated soup bowls and add a tablespoon of sherry to each just before serving.

YIELD: 6 TO 8 SERVINGS

ONION SOUP

¼ cup unsalted butter
3 medium onions, thinly
   sliced
1 clove garlic, minced
Salt and freshly ground
   pepper, to taste
1 tablespoon flour
6 cups beef stock or
   consomme
1 cup port or full-bodied
   Burgundy
½ bay leaf
¼ teaspoon thyme
2 teaspoons Dijon mustard
6 slices French bread
½ cup freshly grated
   Parmesan cheese
½ cup grated Gruyere or
   Swiss cheese

Melt butter in a saute pan over medium heat and cook
onions and garlic until tender and transparent. Do not
overcook. Sprinkle with salt, pepper, and flour. Stir to
thicken.

In a pot, heat stock, wine, bay leaf, and thyme. Add onions
and garlic and bring to a light boil. Reduce heat, cover, and
simmer 30 minutes. Stir in mustard. Flavor of soup is
improved if refrigerated overnight at this point.

To serve, allow soup to stand at room temperature for at
least 30 minutes. Preheat oven to 450 degrees. Pour soup
into ovenproof bowls or crocks and place a slice of toasted
and buttered French bread on each. Cover with grated
cheeses, and bake until cheese is golden and thoroughly
melted.

YIELD: 6 SERVINGS

*Wine is added to some soup
recipes for its flavor or
aroma, not for the alcohol,
which generally dissipates
when cooked. Use a quality
wine and avoid "cooking"
wines. These products are
inferior in flavor, and if they
actually contain alcohol, they
are made undrinkable with
strongly flavored additives
that can wreck a recipe.*

FRESH TOMATO SOUP

2 tablespoons olive oil
2 tablespoons unsalted
  butter
3 young leeks, sliced with
  tops removed
4 sprigs fresh thyme,
  chopped (or ½ teaspoon
  dried)
4 leaves fresh basil,
  chopped (or ½ teaspoon
  dried)
2½ pounds ripe tomatoes,
  seeded
3 tablespoons tomato paste
Salt and freshly ground
  pepper, to taste
¼ cup flour
4 cups chicken broth
1 teaspoon sugar
1 cup cream (optional)
Croutons (garnish)

To make croutons: Cube day-old sourdough bread brushed with butter. Bake at 375 degrees until lightly browned and crisp. Remove from oven and while still warm, place in a bag with freshly grated Parmesan cheese and your favorite herb combination, shake gently and cool. Store in an airtight container.

Heat oil and butter in a heavy kettle. Add leeks, thyme, and basil. Cook until leeks are transparent and remove from heat.

Puree tomatoes, with skins, and add to kettle. Add tomato paste, salt, and pepper. Return to medium-low heat and stir. Simmer uncovered for about 10 minutes.

In a small mixing bowl, combine flour and five table-spoons of chicken broth. Whisk to blend, then stir into kettle. Add remaining broth. Simmer for a half hour, stirring frequently. Stir in sugar and add cream gradually. Do not boil.

Soup is ready to serve when cream is thoroughly heated. Pour soup into bowls and sprinkle with croutons. Serve immediately.

YIELD: 6 SERVINGS

FISHERMAN'S WHARF FISH STEW

Food Editor Antonia Allegra sends this recipe from Carmel Berman Reingold, author of *California Cuisine*. Fresh fish recommended for this stew are Pacific ling cod, Pacific snapper, red snapper, sea bass, salmon, or a combination of two or more.

4 tablespoons olive oil
4 tablespoons butter
1 large onion, chopped
2 cloves garlic, pressed
8 tomatoes, peeled and chopped
6 ounces tomato paste
1 red or green bell pepper, seeded, cored, and chopped
1 teaspoon fresh basil
1 teaspoon fresh oregano
1 bay leaf

½ teaspoon red pepper flakes, crushed (or less, to taste)
3 cups dry white or red wine
2 pounds fresh fish, cut into large pieces
½ pound fresh scallops
12 to 15 clams, thoroughly scrubbed, unshelled
10 to 12 ounces fresh crab, cracked (Dungeness preferred)

Heat oil and butter in a large pot. Saute onion and garlic for three minutes or until onion is transparent. Add tomatoes and tomato paste and cook, stirring until all ingredients are warm. Add bell pepper, seasonings, and wine. Stir to combine and cover. Simmer over low heat 30 minutes.

Add fish and cook 15 minutes. Add shellfish and cook an additional 15 minutes or until all the fish is cooked and the clams have opened. Correct seasoning and serve at once.

YIELD: 6 TO 8 SERVINGS

CREAM OF ARTICHOKE MUSHROOM SOUP

Use of packaged (frozen or canned) artichokes makes this recipe easier to prepare; however, for the best flavor, fresh artichokes in season are preferred.

3 tablespoons unsalted butter
¼ cup chopped scallions, bulbs only
1 cup thinly sliced fresh mushrooms
2 tablespoons flour
1 cup chicken broth
1 cup cream
1½ cups half and half
1½ cups artichokes, sliced
1 teaspoon lemon juice
Cayenne or dash of Tabasco, to taste
Salt and freshly ground pepper, to taste
Scallion tops and thinly sliced lemon rounds (garnish)

California's coast around Castroville grows an incredible number of artichokes, which thrive in the cool, foggy climate. Artichokes are available all year, but peak in March to May. An unusual quality artichokes possess, other than their odd shape and fuzzy chokes, is that they make other foods, eaten at the same time, taste sweeter than they would otherwise.

In a stock pot or large saucepan, melt butter over medium heat and saute scallions and mushrooms until tender. Do not overcook. Add flour, stirring gently for about two minutes. Add broth, cream, and half and half in small amounts at a time, keeping temperature constant. Whisk over low heat to thicken. Stir in artichokes, lemon juice, and seasonings.

To serve, pour soup into warmed serving bowls and top with a lemon slice. Scallion brushes can be made by snipping scallion tops into a dozen two- to three-inch pieces. Slice each on one side to open flat and make vertical slices, leaving a portion at the top intact. Gently fan and add to soup as garnish.

YIELD: 6 SERVINGS

HEARTY SEAFOOD SOUP

4 links hot sausage
1 large onion, chopped
1 clove garlic
2 stalks celery, chopped
1 whole pepperoni, sliced
4 large ripe tomatoes,
  peeled and coarsely
  chopped
4 ounces tomato paste
1 cup red wine
2 bay leaves
2 tablespoons chopped
  fresh basil

4 tablespoons chopped
  fresh parsley
¼ teaspoon thyme
¼ teaspoon rosemary
1 small red chili, seeded
  and chopped
Freshly ground pepper,
  to taste
6 jumbo shrimp, peeled
  and deveined
12 ounces red snapper, cut
  into large pieces

In a skillet, cook sausage until browned and set aside to drain. Pour off all but two to three tablespoons of fat, reduce heat, and saute onion, garlic, and celery until transparent.

Chop sausage and combine in a large pot with onion, garlic, celery, pepperoni, tomatoes, tomato paste, and wine. Simmer over medium heat for 10 minutes. Add herbs, chili, and pepper. Water may be added at this point to thin broth, if desired. Cover and simmer over low heat for 20 to 30 minutes. Add shrimp and fish and cook an additional hour. Flavor is enhanced if soup is prepared in advance. Remove bay leaves before serving.

YIELD: 4 TO 6 SERVINGS

Tomatoes were once touted as an aphrodisiac and once thought of as poisonous, rather exciting reputations for a fruit that has become boring from mass production. Tomatoes just don't develop adequate flavor and vitamins unless allowed to ripen on the vine. Seek out locally grown tomatoes. They may not be as "pretty," but beauty, of course, is only skin deep.

OYSTER STEW

5 tablespoons unsalted
  butter
1½ cups minced onion
2 stalks celery, minced
2 cloves garlic, minced
6 cups chicken stock
2 cups oysters
5 tablespoons flour
1 cup milk
1 cup light cream
¼ teaspoon white pepper
¼ teaspoon Worcestershire
  sauce
4 tablespoons chopped
  fresh Italian parsley
Paprika, to taste

A substitution for light cream is 7/8 cup of whole milk with three tablespoons of butter added.

Melt two tablespoons of butter in a large saute pan and add onions, celery, and garlic. Cook until tender and drain off butter. Heat four cups chicken stock in a large pot. Add onion mixture and bring to a slow boil.

In a saucepan, bring remaining stock to a boil and add oysters. Cook five minutes, pour off stock into pot with onions, and allow oysters to cool slightly. Chop oysters and set aside.

Melt remaining butter in a saute pan, add flour slowly, stirring constantly. Add milk and cream slowly, stirring until sauce thickens. Do not boil. Stir this sauce into pot. Add oysters, pepper, Worcestershire sauce, and parsley. Heat through but do not boil. To serve, pour stew into warm bowls, sprinkle with paprika, and garnish with parsley sprigs, if desired.

YIELD: 8 SERVINGS

TORTILLA SOUP

10 corn tortillas
1 cup peanut oil
¼ teaspoon paprika
¼ teaspoon chili powder
¼ teaspoon salt
2 quarts vegetable stock
  (or water)
1 onion, finely chopped
½ cup tomato puree
2 tablespoons salsa
1 tablespoon chopped fresh
  cilantro
¾ cup shredded Jack
  cheese
¾ cup shredded Cheddar
  cheese
2 ripe avocados, sliced
Sour cream and salsa
  (garnish)
1 lime, cut into 6 wedges

Slice tortillas in quarter-inch strips and allow to dry out several hours until leathery. Heat oil in skillet and fry strips until crisp. Drain on paper towels. Combine paprika, chili powder, and salt. Sprinkle over hot chips.

Combine the stock, onion, tomato puree, salsa, and cilantro in a saucepan. Simmer over medium heat for 20 minutes or until onion is tender.

To serve, place cheese and a few tortilla strips in the bottom of heated soup bowls. Ladle in hot soup. Garnish with an avocado slice and a small dollop of sour cream topped with a dollop of salsa. Serve lime wedges, salsa, avocado, and chopped cilantro in separate dishes for additional toppings. Place extra tortilla strips in a basket and serve with soup.

YIELD: 6 SERVINGS

MAMA GHIO'S SHELLFISH CIOPPINO

Anthony's Restaurant sends us an all-time favorite.

Sauce:

¼ cup olive oil
½ cup butter
1 large onion, chopped
3 tablespoons chopped
  fresh parsley
4 cloves garlic, chopped
¾ cup sherry
2 cups chopped plum
  tomatoes
1 cup tomato sauce
2 bay leaves
1 teaspoon salt
½ teaspooon freshly
  ground pepper
Dash Tabasco
½ teaspoon dried thyme
2 cups water

Seafood:

1 fresh Dungeness crab
2 lobster tails
8 large shrimp, unshelled
12 clams, in the shell
½ pound fresh scallops
½ pound halibut fillets

Heat oil and butter in a large pot. Add onion, parsley, and garlic and cook until onion is transparent. Add sherry and cook an additional five minutes. Add tomatoes and tomato sauce, bay leaves and seasonings. Stir frequently while cooking 15 to 20 minutes. Add water, cover, and simmer for a half hour.

Add all seafood except halibut to the sauce. Add more water if necessary. Cook for five minutes, add halibut, and cook an additional ten minutes. When clams have opened, cioppino is ready to serve.

YIELD: 4 SERVINGS

SOPA DE FRIJOLES

The rich, hearty flavor of this soup improves when prepared a day in advance and refrigerated. Substitute peanut or safflower oil for the lard if a quality lard is not available. Commercial white lards are not recommended— not only do these lards lack flavor, but they are made fluffy with stabilizers.

2 cups pinto beans
8 cups water
1 clove garlic, peeled
1 large onion, cut in chunks
1 sprig epazote or cilantro
1 tablespoon good quality lard
1 tablespoon salt
4 seedless chilies pasillas, or fewer to taste
1 tablespoon peanut oil

2 ripe tomatoes
1 clove garlic, peeled
1 medium onion, cut in chunks
2 tablespoons lard
5 to 6 cups chicken stock
1 cup Cheddar or Jack cheese, cubed
8 small slices avocado, sour cream, tortilla chips (garnish)

Rinse and pick through beans to remove bad ones, small stones, or husks. Bring water to a boil in a large pot and add beans. Turn off heat, cover pot, and allow beans to sit for one hour. Reheat to medium, add garlic clove, onion, and epazote and continue cooking beans for 30 minutes. Add lard and salt and cook until tender. Remove from heat and allow to cool. Puree beans and the liquid in batches and set aside.

Fry chilies in oil until they soften, being careful not to burn them. Puree chilies, tomatoes, garlic, and onion. Heat lard in large saucepan and fry chili mixture for five minutes. Add bean puree and simmer an additional ten minutes. Pour bean and chili mixture into pot and add enough chicken stock for a thick soup consistency. Season with salt and simmer for ten minutes.

To serve, place cheese in the bottom of warmed soup bowls and pour on hot soup. Garnish with a dollop of sour cream, a small slice of avocado, and tortilla chips.

YIELD: 8 SERVINGS

According to one source, dried beans shouldn't be soaked ahead of time, nor should salt be added to the cooking water until beans are almost done—it hardens the skins. Beans taste better if cooked a day ahead, but they should be refrigerated to avoid becoming sour. When cooked, they can be frozen.

Epazote, or "Mexican tea," is a flavorful Mexican herb that also grows in the United States. The Mexican-grown variety is usually stronger in taste. (If unavailable, oregano can be substituted.) The herb supposedly reduces those notorious gassy effects associated with beans.

MEXICAN LENTIL SOUP

This recipe doubles well, and any extra soup can be frozen. Ham hocks can be substituted for baked ham. Add two hocks to the lentils as they cook and remove them before pureeing the mixture.

6 cups chicken broth
3 cups water
2 cups lentils
4 bay leaves
¼ cup coarsely chopped
  garlic cloves
1½ cups chopped celery
1½ cups chopped carrots
1½ cups green chili salsa
1 large white onion,
  chopped
2 cups chopped baked ham
2 tablespoons chopped
  fresh basil
½ teaspoon cracked black
  pepper
¼ cup yellow corn meal
Sour cream and fresh
  cilantro (garnish)

Bring three cups broth and three cups water to a boil in a large pot. Add lentils, bay leaves, and garlic. Reduce heat, cover, and simmer for 20 minutes. Add remaining ingredients except corn meal and the reserve broth. Bring to a boil, reduce heat, and simmer covered for 30 minutes. Stir in corn meal and cook an additional 15 minutes or until vegetables are tender but not overcooked. Remove from heat and allow to cool.

Puree the mixture in batches. Heat reserve stock and stir in puree. Serve in warmed soup bowls and garnish with a dollop of sour cream and sprigs of cilantro.

The soup will thicken as it cools because of the corn meal. When reheated it returns to its original consistency. Additional broth or water can be added to achieve desired thickness.

YIELD: 8 SERVINGS

CREAM OF SEA URCHIN ROE SOUP

Chairman of the board of the La Jolla chapter of the International Food and Wine Society of London. That long title is only the beginning of a long list of honors that profiles Ed Muzzy, past president of Almaden Winery. With his wife Helene, he shares a well-known association with exceptional food and wine. And they share with us this special recipe.

2 cups clam broth
1 cup milk
½ cup unsalted butter, softened
Coral roe from a whole sea urchin
2 tablespoons cornstarch
10 drops Tabasco
1 teaspoon thyme
Salt and freshly ground white pepper, to taste
6 ounces dry white wine

Heat broth and milk, but do not boil. Place half the mixture in a blender and add remaining ingredients except wine. Blend well. Pour into a saucepan with remaining broth mixture. Simmer gently five minutes, add wine, and remove from heat. Adjust seasoning.

YIELD: 4 TO 6 SERVINGS

VEGETABLE PESTO SOUP

Pesto adds zip to this heart-warming favorite.

3 medium potatoes,
  unpeeled,
  or ¼ pound spaghettini
½ pound fresh green beans
3 carrots, unpeeled
1 medium onion
2 quarts stock
1 tablespoon salt
¼ teaspoon pepper
½ pound zucchini
16 ounces kidney beans,
  with liquid

Pesto:

4 cloves garlic
6 ounces tomato paste
3 tablespoons chopped
  fresh basil
½ cup freshly grated
  Parmesan cheese
½ cup chopped fresh
  parsley
¼ cup olive oil

Cut potatoes into half-inch cubes (or break spaghettini into two-inch pieces and cook), break beans into half-inch pieces, slice carrots, and chop onions. Add vegetables to stock with salt and pepper. (If using pasta, do not add to stock until after vegetables have cooked.) Bring to a boil, cover and simmer ten minutes. Slice zucchini and add, with kidney beans, to stock. Cover and simmer ten minutes or until all vegetables are tender.

To make pesto, combine all ingredients, except olive oil, in a blender or food processor. Process until very finely chopped. Add oil gradually, a teaspoon at a time, until mixture resembles a thick sauce.

Stir pesto into hot soup just before serving, or add a heaping tablespoon to individual bowls. Garnish each bowl with vegetable slices and a sprinkle of parsley.

YIELD: 6 SERVINGS

AVOCADOS WITH MUSHROOM FILLING

6 ripe avocados
Juice of 1 lemon
¾ cup olive oil
¼ cup tarragon vinegar
1 teaspoon sugar
½ teaspoon salt
Dash Tabasco
2 hard-cooked eggs, sieved
1 tablespoon chopped fresh
  chives
1 tablespoon chopped fresh
  parsley
1 tablespoon dry mustard
½ teaspoon Worcestershire
  sauce
1 pound mushrooms, sliced
Lettuce leaves

Cut avocados in half lengthwise and remove pits. With a large spoon, scoop fruit from peel in one piece. Drizzle with lemon juice. Chop one avocado into small pieces.

In a saucepan, combine oil, vinegar, sugar, salt, and Tabasco. Bring to a boil and remove from heat immediately. Stir in eggs, chives, parsley, mustard, and Worcestershire sauce. Check seasonings.

Mix mushrooms and chopped avocado together in a bowl. Pour in dressing and toss well. Place avocado halves on lettuce leaves. Fill with mushroom mixture and serve.

YIELD: 5 OR 10 SERVINGS

To "peel" an avocado quickly and easily, insert a sharp knife through the skin at the bulbous end and make a vertical slice (to the pit) down to the stalk end. Do the same for the other side. Pull avocado halves apart and remove the pit. Fruit can be removed in one piece from the skin by inserting a spoon at one end and scooping out the flesh.

ENDIVE AND MUSHROOM SALAD

The understated flavors of endive and mushrooms are the perfect background for this delicious vinaigrette.

½ pound Belgian endive
½ pound fresh mushrooms
⅓ cup chopped walnuts
2 tablespoons fresh Italian
 parsley, chopped

Vinaigrette:

2 tablespoons white wine
 vinegar
1 teaspoon lemon juice
Salt and freshly ground
 pepper, to taste
Dijon mustard, to taste
3 tablespoons olive oil
2 tablespoons thick cream

Belgian endive's slightly bitter flavor and crunchiness complement milder greens in salads. These small, opalescent heads should be tightly furled, have no marks or dark spots, and leaves should be firm. Buy heads that are wrapped, not the ones out on display, because exposure to light reduces freshness.

Rinse endive in very cold water and dry gently with paper towels. Cut in half lengthwise and break leaves apart. Trim bases and cut into large bitesize pieces.

Clean mushrooms and slice horizontally across caps to stems. (Set stems aside for some other use.) Stack several caps and cut into julienne slices. Add to endive in a salad bowl. Sprinkle on walnuts and parsley.

In a small bowl, combine vinegar, lemon juice, salt, pepper, and mustard, mixing well. Whisk in oil gradually until an emulsion is formed. Slowly whisk in cream. Pour over salad and toss well before serving.

YIELD: 2 TO 4 SERVINGS

BASQUE BEAN SALAD

This bean salad is an excellent first course for grilled or barbecued meat entrees. Note that the beans should be marinated several hours before serving.

1 pound small white beans
1 onion, peeled and
  quartered
1 large carrot, cut into
  large pieces

Marinade:

⅓ cup thinly sliced
  scallions and tops
2 cloves garlic, minced
¼ cup chopped fresh
  Italian parsley
¼ teaspoon dried oregano
¾ red wine vinegar
¾ cup safflower oil
½ cup olive oil
1 teaspoon salt
½ teaspoon freshly ground
  pepper

Romaine lettuce and bean
  sprouts

Cook beans in 2½ quarts water with onion and carrots until beans are tender. Drain, discard carrot and onion, and rinse beans with cool water.

Whisk together marinade ingredients. While beans are still warm, pour the mixture over the beans, stir, and marinate covered for at least six hours in the refrigerator.

Serve on a bed of romaine and sprouts. Garnish with slices of sun-dried tomatoes and toasted sunflower seeds, if desired.

YIELD: 6 TO 8 SERVINGS

MARINATED MUSHROOM SALAD

The marinade for this recipe also works well with tomatoes, artichoke hearts, and shrimp. For the best result, allow mushrooms to marinate overnight.

1 pound fresh mushrooms
Leaves of romaine or
**   red-leaf lettuce**

Marinade:

6 tablespoons olive oil
¼ cup red wine vinegar
1 teaspoon freshly ground
**   pepper**
1½ teaspoons salt
1 clove garlic, slivered
Dash Tabasco or cayenne
2 tablespoons chopped
**   fresh basil**
2 tablespoons chopped
**   fresh parsley**
3 scallions and tops,
**   thinly sliced**

Pow! One innovative cook we know adds Tabasco, with sound effects, to just about any recipe that could use a punch of flavor. Tabasco is a liquid pepper sauce that has been aged and bottled. Made from very hot chilies, it substitutes well for cayenne.

Rinse mushrooms and dry with paper towels. Brush or wipe the caps and trim the stems. Rinse, dry, and crisp lettuce leaves in the refrigerator.

Mix the marinade ingredients in a jar and shake well. Place mushrooms in a bowl and pour in marinade, being sure to cover all mushrooms. Let stand covered at room temperature for four to five hours, tossing occasionally. Refrigerate overnight.

To serve, remove mushrooms from refrigerator, toss, and allow to stand at room temperature at least 30 minutes. Place mushrooms on lettuce leaves on chilled salad plates. Add a drizzle of marinade if desired.

YIELD: 4 SERVINGS

TOMATOES WITH DILL AND FETA CHEESE

A refreshing salad for summer's warmer days. Reserve dressing may be used for other fresh garden delights—sliced cucumbers and baby scallions, or blanched snow peas and sliced sweet peppers.

1 cup diced feta cheese
½ cup plain yogurt
½ cup milk
1 tablespoon fresh dill,
  minced
3 large ripe tomatoes,
  cut in small wedges
1 head butter lettuce
Dill sprigs (garnish)

Combine cheese, yogurt, milk, and dill and blend well until smooth. Refrigerate.

Arrange tomatoes on leaves of rinsed and crisped lettuce. Pour dressing over tomatoes and top with dill sprigs. Refrigerate reserve dressing and use within two to three days.

YIELD: 6 SERVINGS

FRESH GREEN BEAN SALAD

½ pound green beans
½ pound fresh mushrooms
1 cup walnuts
½ cup chopped parsley
Juice of 1 lemon
½ teaspoon salt
Freshly ground black
  pepper, to taste
½ cup olive oil

Pepper is the most used spice in the world and the United States is the largest importer. Peppercorns differ in aroma and flavor depending on species and cultivation. The moment a peppercorn is broken, the volatile flavor-holding properties begin to dissipate. In general, our recipes call for freshly ground pepper—the difference between this and preground pepper is beyond comparison. Add fresh pepper to taste; the intensity can vary.

Trim tips from beans and slice down the centers. Bring a large pot of salted water to a boil, drop in beans, and cook just until tender. Drain and place immediately under cold running water to stop cooking and retain color. Drain further in a colander. Refrigerate.

Clean mushrooms and trim stems. Slice horizontally across the caps, stack, and cut into julienned pieces. Toast walnuts on a baking sheet for ten minutes in a 350-degree oven. Remove to a cold plate.

Place beans in a large glass serving bowl. Layer the mushrooms on top and follow with walnuts and parsley. Add lemon juice followed by salt and pepper. Pour oil over the top and let stand, allowing flavors to combine. Toss before serving.

YIELD: 4 SERVINGS

ASPARAGUS WITH LEMON HERB DRESSING

Here's a salad that isn't served cold. Doing so would inhibit the subtle and elegant flavors.

1 pound fresh early asparagus spears
3 tablespoons pine nuts, toasted
¼ cup olive oil
1 tablespoon fresh lemon juice
1 clove garlic, mashed

½ teaspoon oregano, crumbled
2 tablespoons fresh chopped basil
¼ teaspoon salt
Freshly ground black pepper, to taste

Remove ends and any tough scales from asparagus. Steam very briefly, until spears are crisp tender. Drain.

Whisk together remaining ingredients and heat in a non-aluminum pan. Toss asparagus with dressing. Place spears on a serving dish and sprinkle with pine nuts. Cool to room temperature and serve immediately.

YIELD: 4 SERVINGS

CUCUMBER MINT SALAD

Juice of 1 lemon
½ cup sour cream
½ cup plain yogurt
¼ cup fresh mint, chopped
¼ teaspoon salt
½ cup golden raisins

2 large cucumbers
2 green apples
1 pound fresh spinach, rinsed and trimmed of stems
Sprigs of mint (garnish)

Combine half the lemon juice with sour cream, yogurt, mint, salt, and raisins. (Raisins can be coarsely chopped if desired.) Mix well. Peel and slice cucumbers very thin. Add cucumbers to sour cream mixture and chill thoroughly.

Core and slice apples. Toss slices in reserved lemon juice. Place spinach leaves on chilled salad plates and top with cucumber mixture. Garnish with mint and place apple slices on the side.

YIELD: 6 SERVINGS

BROCCOLI VINAIGRETTE

Broccoli isn't the only vegetable this vinaigrette perks up. Young fresh green beans or baby asparagus, slightly blanched, also make delicious salads.

2 pounds fresh broccoli

Vinaigrette:

1½ teaspoons salt
1 teaspoon freshly ground
  black pepper
¼ teaspoon sugar
½ teaspoon dry mustard
1 teaspoon Dijon mustard
2 cloves garlic, minced
5 tablespoons red wine
  vinegar
⅔ cup olive oil
1 raw egg, beaten
½ cup light cream
1 tablespoon each of finely
  chopped chives, parsley,
  olives, and capers
  (garnish)

Consider cooking or blanching salad vegetables without salt added to the boiling water. Add a pinch or more of sugar instead. The vegetables will have a finished flavor but one that isn't sweet.

Cut broccoli florets into bitesize serving pieces. Peel and slice edible portions of the stems with a sharp knife. Add a generous pinch of sugar and salt to a large pot of water and bring to a boil. Add broccoli and parboil one minute until it turns bright green. Drain and rinse with cold running water until broccoli has cooled. Drain further in a colander. Refrigerate.

Combine vinaigrette ingredients and mix well (or shake in a jar) until smooth. Refrigerate for several hours to allow flavors to blend. Arrange broccoli on serving plates and pour on dressing one hour before serving. Garnish.

YIELD: APPROXIMATELY 6 SERVINGS

BANANA CURRY SALAD

3 bananas, firm but ripe
1 to 2 tablespoons freshly
  squeezed lemon juice
2 cups cooked white rice,
  cooled
1 cup seedless grapes
½ cup julienned celery
2 tablespoons chopped
  chives
2 tablespoons chopped
  pimientos
½ cup unsalted peanuts

Dressing:

1 cup mayonnaise
2 tablespoons heavy cream
1 tablespoon fresh lemon
  juice
1 tablespoon curry powder
1 teaspoon dry mustard
1 head red-leaf lettuce
Condiments: toasted
  coconut, toasted sun-
  flower seeds, chutney,
  raisins (golden and
  black), peanuts

Slice bananas and sprinkle with lemon juice to cover all pieces. Set aside. Combine rice, grapes, celery, chives, pimientos, and peanuts in a large bowl. Gently fold in bananas and refrigerate.

Prepare dressing a couple of hours in advance to allow flavors to blend. For best results, use homemade mayonnaise (see recipe on page 134). Whisk together mayonnaise, cream, lemon juice, curry, and mustard. Refrigerate. Pour dressing over salad and toss gently. Serve on lettuce leaves with condiments on the side.

YIELD: 4 SERVINGS

Bananas ripen off the plant and can be bought at various stages of ripeness to suit individual taste. To ripen bananas "quickly," store them in a paper bag in a dark warm closet.

COBB SALAD VARIATION

Dressing:

½ cup olive oil
½ cup white wine vinegar
½ teaspoon salt
2 teaspoons sugar
¾ teaspoon freshly ground
   pepper
1¼ teaspoons dry mustard
1 clove garlic, minced
⅓ cup minced parsley

Salad:

3 whole chicken breasts
½ pound bacon
3 small heads butter lettuce
2 large ripe tomatoes, diced
2 avocados, sliced and
   drizzled with lemon juice
8 ounces blue cheese

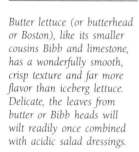

Butter lettuce (or butterhead or Boston), like its smaller cousins Bibb and limestone, has a wonderfully smooth, crisp texture and far more flavor than iceberg lettuce. Delicate, the leaves from butter or Bibb heads will wilt readily once combined with acidic salad dressings.

Combine dressing ingredients, blending well. Refrigerate several hours.

Wrap chicken in foil, set in baking pan, and bake 40 minutes at 500 degrees. Remove from oven and allow to cool before unwrapping. Remove skin and bones from chicken and slice into strips.

Cook bacon until crispy, drain, and break into pieces. Rinse and dry lettuce and tear leaves into bitesize pieces. Place in a large, shallow salad bowl. Arrange chicken, bacon, tomatoes, avocado, and cheese in bands across top of lettuce. At the table, pour dressing on salad and toss well.

YIELD: 6 SERVINGS

FENNEL SALAD

2 zucchini, julienned
2 fennel bulbs, trimmed
  and sliced
2 tomatoes, thinly sliced

Vinaigrette:

3 tablespoons red wine
  vinegar
¼ teaspoon salt
¼ teaspoon freshly ground
  pepper
1 clove garlic, minced
½ cup olive oil

Sprinkle salt on zucchini slices and set aside to drain. Blanch the fennel slices in boiling water for a minute or two. Drain and rinse with cold water immediately. Drain further in a colander. Place tomato slices on a serving platter, top with fennel, and set aside.

To prepare vinaigrette, whisk together vinegar, salt, pepper, and garlic, and gradually whisk in oil until well blended.

Squeeze excess liquid from zucchini. Add zucchini to vinaigrette. Pour this mixture over the tomato and fennel. Cover platter and refrigerate allowing flavors to blend an hour or more before serving.

YIELD: 4 SERVINGS

RADISH SALAD

That stimulating peppery taste of radish has garnished many a salad, but here it's the main attraction. Because radishes are available year-round, this is a salad for all seasons.

2 cups diced radish
¾ cup cubed Gruyere or
   Swiss cheese
2 scallions and tops,
   chopped
⅓ cup mayonnaise
½ teaspoon Dijon mustard
1 tablespoon sour cream
Romaine lettuce, rinsed and
   crisped

When selecting radishes, pinch them to check firmness and avoid bunches with yellowed leaves or with bulbs that aren't smooth and crisp. Chilled radishes will stay fresh for about a week. Remove the tops to prevent the leaves from taking moisture from the bulbs, but consider using the leaves— they supposedly aid digestion.

Toss together radish, cheese, and scallions, reserving a few chopped greens for garnish. Combine mayonnaise, mustard, and sour cream together in a small bowl, mixing well. Add to radish mixture, being sure to coat all pieces. Cover and refrigerate allowing flavors to blend. To serve, spoon salad onto romaine leaves and sprinkle with chopped greens.

(This salad might also be used as a canape topping or as the filling for a grilled sourdough sandwich with melted Gruyere cheese.)

YIELD: 4 SERVINGS

SPINACH AND STRAWBERRY SALAD

2 pounds fresh spinach
1 to 2 pints fresh
strawberries

Dressing:

⅓ **cup sugar**
1½ **teaspoons minced**
onion
¼ **teaspoon paprika**
¼ **teaspoon Worcestershire**
sauce
½ **cup safflower oil**
3 to 4 tablespoons cider
vinegar
2 tablespoons sesame seeds
1 tablespoon poppy seeds

Wash and dry spinach. Remove stems and tear into large pieces. Pick through strawberries to select ripe and un-damaged berries. Rinse, remove stems, and cut in half.

Whisk or blend together sugar, onion, paprika, and Worcestershire sauce. Gradually add oil and vinegar in a steady stream until well blended. Check seasoning. Stir in seeds.

To serve, arrange spinach and strawberries on chilled serving plates. Drizzle dressing over the top.

YIELD: 6 TO 8 SERVINGS

GREENS AND VARIATIONS

The ingredients for this recipe can easily be altered or substituted with other salad favorites.

Dressing:

1 egg yolk
1½ teaspoons dry mustard
⅓ cup red wine vinegar
1 cup walnut or olive oil
¼ teaspoon freshly ground
   pepper
1 tablespoon lemon juice
½ teaspoon Worcestershire
   sauce

Salad:

6 cups salad greens
1 cup hearts of palm,
   drained and coarsely
   chopped
1 cup artichoke hearts,
   cut up
⅓ cup bacon, cooked and
   crumbled
⅔ cup blue cheese,
   crumbled
⅓ cup chopped walnuts
⅓ cup chopped chives

Red wine vinegar can be made from a variety of full-bodied wines. For dressings, it combines well with olive oil or nut oils. The flavor is sharp and sweet, heavier than other vinegars, making it a good choice for very tangy or bitter greens. White wine vinegar, like white wine, is generally lighter and sweeter. For a mild dressing better suited to delicate greens or fruits, mix this vinegar with oils that have little to no flavor.

To prepare the dressing, whisk together egg yolk, dry mustard, and vinegar in a stainless steel bowl. Gradually whisk in the oil, followed by pepper, lemon juice, and Worcestershire sauce. Be sure ingredients are well mixed. Cover bowl and let stand at room temperature for at least 30 minutes before serving.

Rinse salad greens and crisp in the refrigerator. To serve, pour half the dressing in a large bowl. Add greens, hearts of palm, and artichoke hearts. Toss. Place salad on chilled plates and sprinkle each with bacon, cheese, and walnuts. Drizzle with remaining dressing to taste and top with chives.

YIELD: 6 SERVINGS

SUMMER TOMATO PASTA SALAD

Best if prepared in advance.

4 pounds ripe tomatoes
12 ounces marinated
  artichoke hearts
½ cup olive oil
2 cups coarsely chopped
  onions
4 cloves garlic, peeled and
  chopped
¼ cup chopped fresh basil
½ tablespoon dried oregano
½ cup chopped Italian
  parsley
1 dried red pepper, crushed
2 tablespoons whole black
  peppercorns
1 teaspoon salt
¼ cup freshly grated
  Romano cheese
4 pounds cheese-filled
  tortellini

Blanch and peel tomatoes. Cut in half and squeeze out seeds and juice. Chop coarsely and set aside. Drain artichokes and reserve marinade.

Heat oil in a large saucepan and saute onions, garlic, basil, oregano, parsley, and red pepper for five minutes over medium heat. Crush peppercorns and add to mixture. Add tomatoes and salt. Simmer uncovered over medium heat for about an hour. Add reserved marinade and simmer, stirring often, for 30 minutes. Reduce heat, stir in artichokes, and simmer until sauce is thick, another half hour. Stir in Romano cheese. Remove from heat.

Cook pasta in boiling water until just tender. Drain in a colander and immediately douse with cold water to stop cooking. Add pasta to sauce and allow to cool. Refrigerate overnight for best flavor. Before serving, allow pasta to stand at room temperature at least 30 minutes.

YIELD: 8 TO 12 SERVINGS

Sweet basil, long considered a love charm in Italy, has a minty, clovelike aroma and a pungent taste. A purple variety, opal basil, is occasionally available and is similar in flavor to the green basil. Its deep purple is a wonderful color addition when whole leaves are included in salads or used as a garnish. Sweet and opal basil wilt easily, so buy firm bunches and keep the stems moist when refrigerated. Both varieties can be frozen for later use in cooked dishes. Coat the leaves with oil, or just rinse them, and pack in an airtight container to freeze.

FETTUCCINE SALAD WITH ROASTED PEPPERS AND SHRIMP

1 pound fettuccine
¼ cup Italian parsley,
  chopped
1 clove garlic, minced
¾ cup corn oil
⅓ cup white wine vinegar
½ teaspoon salt
½ teaspoon dry mustard
¼ teaspoon freshly ground
  white pepper

Pinch sugar
3 medium sweet red
  peppers
3 fresh poblano chilies
1 pound fresh shrimp
1 pound young zucchini
½ cup pine nuts
8 ounces feta cheese,
  crumbled
Cilantro sprigs (garnish)

Cook pasta in boiling water until just tender. Drain thoroughly and set aside in a large salad bowl. Combine parsley, garlic, oil, vinegar, salt, mustard, pepper, and sugar, mixing well. Pour half of this mixture over the pasta and toss to cover pieces. Reserve remaining dressing.

Roast the peppers on all sides under broiler (or use a long fork and hold peppers over a gas flame, turning until the skins are evenly darkened). Put peppers in a closed paper bag for 10 to 15 minutes (or in a plastic bag in the freezer). Peel the skins and split peppers open to remove stems, seeds, and veins. Cut into strips, pat dry, and add to the pasta. Roast and prepare the chilies in the same manner but leave the veins. (Use rubber gloves when handling chilies.)

Boil the shrimp until just cooked through, about three to four minutes. Immediately douse in cold water. Drain, peel, and devein. Cut shrimp in half lengthwise and add to pasta. Shred zucchini, drain on paper towels, then add to pasta.

Heat two tablespoons of the reserved dressing in a small skillet over medium heat. Add pine nuts and stir until golden brown. Remove from pan with slotted spoon and drain on paper towels.

Pour remaining dressing over the pasta mixture, add cheese and pine nuts and toss well. Serve on individual salad plates and garnish with sprigs of cilantro.

YIELD: 6 SERVINGS

SMOKED SALMON PASTA SALAD

Smoked albacore, when available in fish markets, is an excellent substitute for the salmon. Salmon marinated in soy sauce and barbecue-grilled is also a tasty option. Be sure it has cooled thoroughly before including in this recipe.

1 pound spinach noodles
Juice of 1 lemon
½ cup olive oil
1 pound smoked salmon
1 cup sour cream
½ cup plain yogurt
3 tablespoons fresh
  chopped dill
1 tablespoon lemon juice
Salt, to taste

Bring pot of water to boil. Add lemon juice and noodles to water. Cook until just tender. Drain, shaking well to remove all water. Place noodles in a large bowl and toss with olive oil. Set aside to cool.

Remove any skin and bones from salmon. Flake and combine with sour cream, yogurt, dill, and lemon juice.

When pasta is completely cool, fold in salmon mixture and add salt to taste. Cover and refrigerate. Let stand 20 to 30 minutes at room temperature before serving.

YIELD: 6 TO 8 SERVINGS

PASTA SALAD WITH SPINACH AND FETA CHEESE

Dressing:

¾ cup olive oil
¾ cup champagne vinegar
3 cloves garlic, minced
2 teaspoons Dijon mustard
½ cup freshly grated
 Parmesan cheese
1 tablespoon minced
 oregano
Salt and freshly ground
 pepper, to taste

Salad:

1 pound pasta shells
 or bows
2 pounds fresh spinach,
 trimmed of stems and
 shredded
3 ripe tomatoes, chopped
1 bunch scallions, finely
 chopped
1 cup feta cheese, crumbled
2 cucumbers, peeled and
 thinly sliced
1 cup pine nuts, toasted

Combine dressing ingredients and blend well. Cook pasta in boiling water until just tender. Drain. Toss with half of the dressing. Set aside to cool.

In a large bowl, combine remaining ingredients and add reserve dressing. Gently toss in cooled pasta. Cover and refrigerate. Toss again before serving.

YIELD: 8 TO 10 SERVINGS

CORN AND RICE SALAD WITH ROASTED PEPPERS

The time it takes to prepare this salad is well spent. Serve it as a delicious introduction to a chicken entree, or add cooked and shredded chicken breast to the salad for a variation. Increase the dressing ingredients by half if meat is added.

Dressing:

2 cloves garlic
½ cup raspberry or red wine vinegar
1 tablespoon Dijon mustard
¼ cup chopped fresh basil
¼ cup chopped fresh parsley
1 tablespoon dried oregano
1 cup olive oil

Salad:

2 sweet red peppers
2 green peppers
5 ears fresh corn
4 scallions and tops, sliced
2 cups grated Swiss cheese
4 cups cooked brown or wild rice
3 avocados

Peel garlic cloves, slice in half lengthwise, and remove internal sprout. Mince. Whisk together garlic, vinegar, mustard, and herbs, adding oil gradually until well blended. Refrigerate.

Roast peppers under broiler (or with a long fork over gas flame) until darkened on all sides. Place in a closed paper bag for 10 to 15 minutes. Slip off skins and split open to remove seeds and veins. Cut into julienne strips.

Husk corn and remove silk. Cook in a large pot of boiling water for about five minutes. Drain and allow to cool. Use a sharp knife to slice kernels from cobs. Combine corn with peppers, scallions, and cheese. Pour on half the dressing and toss well. Add rice and remaining dressing. Mix well and refrigerate.

Before serving, peel and cube avocado and gently toss into salad.

YIELD: 6 TO 8 SERVINGS

Parsley contains calcium, iron, and vitamins A and C, among other elements. Keep it moist and cold. In ancient times, it was thought to prevent inebriation, and many folks today use it to freshen breath after a meal heady with garlic.

PASTA SALAD WITH CHICKEN AND BROCCOLI

Dressing:

⅔ cup olive oil
⅔ cup safflower oil
⅔ cup red wine vinegar
2 cloves garlic, minced
2 tablespoons chopped
  fresh basil
2 tablespoons chopped
  fresh tarragon
1 tablespoon Dijon mustard
½ teaspoon freshly ground
  pepper

Salad:

3 whole boneless chicken
  breasts
1 bunch broccoli
1 pound fusilli pasta
  (or spinach tagliarini)
4 ounces black olives,
  sliced
⅓ cup grated Parmesan
  cheese
½ cup slivered almonds,
  toasted
8 ounces marinated
  artichoke hearts

Some Californians love their olives. Others like to dress them up. Here's how they do it: Rinse off unpitted olives in cold water. Marinate in combinations of high quality olive or nut oils, lemon juice or citrus zest, flavored vinegars, herbs, whole peeled garlic cloves, spices, kosher salt (dash or two), or hot pepper flakes. Experiment and, need we add, enjoy.

Combine dressing ingredients and mix well. Broil chicken, turning once, until cooked. Allow to cool slightly, remove skin, and shred. Pour over enough dressing to lightly coat pieces. Refrigerate.

Remove stem from broccoli and chop florets. Steam slightly or parboil for one minute, drain, and douse immediately with cold water. Drain further in a colander.

Cook pasta in boiling water until just tender. Drain. While noodles are still warm, toss with dressing in a large bowl. Add chicken, broccoli, olives, cheese, and almonds. Add artichokes and half the marinade. Check for desired consistency and add remaining marinade if desired. Toss gently but mix well. Cover and refrigerate. Serve thoroughly chilled.

YIELD: 8 TO 10 SERVINGS

CHICKEN PASTA SALAD

A delicious salad that benefits from advance preparation.

7 ounces cheese Raviolini
3 whole boneless chicken
  breasts, cooked, skinned,
  and shredded
2 scallions and tops,
  chopped
1 cup snow peas, trimmed
  and blanched
1 large celery heart with
  leaves, chopped
1 small cucumber, peeled
  and sliced
2 cups seedless grapes
½ cup raisins, coarsely
  chopped
6 ounces marinated
  artichoke hearts, chopped

Dressing:

⅔ cup mayonnaise or plain
  yogurt
½ cup finely grated
  Parmesan
⅓ cup freshly squeezed
  lemon juice
Reserved marinade from
  artichokes
Salt and freshly ground
  pepper, to taste

Garnish:

½ bunch fresh spinach,
  washed and trimmed of
  stems
2 kiwis peeled and sliced
2 tangerines, sectioned,
  seeds removed

Cook pasta in boiling water until just tender. Drain and cool. Place pasta and remaining salad ingredients in a large bowl. Whisk together dressing ingredients and pour over salad. Toss gently but thoroughly and refrigerate at least four hours or overnight.

To serve, mound salad on spinach leaves and garnish with kiwis and tangerines.

YIELD: 6 TO 8 SERVINGS

SMOKED TURKEY WITH SHALLOT VINAIGRETTE

Vinaigrette:

1 cup corn oil
1 tablespoon olive oil
⅔ cup red wine vinegar
3 tablespoons Dijon
   mustard
2 shallots, peeled and
   minced
½ clove garlic, peeled and
   minced
4 tablespoons chopped
   fresh parsley
4 celery leaves, chopped
½ teaspoon salt
2 to 3 tablespoons honey

Salad:

1 head red-leaf lettuce
2 bunches watercress
½ cup alfalfa or radish
   sprouts
½ pound mushrooms
1 bunch baby carrots
½ pound smoked turkey
   (or chicken)
¼ cup unsalted toasted
   almonds, chopped

We think watercress has just too much personality to be relegated to tea-time sandwiches. At its best, watercress has small round leaves that are smooth and crisp and stems that are crunchy. The peppery flavor makes it a choice salad ingredient.

Prepare vinaigrette by blending all ingredients until smooth and creamy. Cover and refrigerate allowing flavors to blend.

Rinse, drain, and tear lettuce into large pieces. Place around perimeter of chilled salad plates. Before untying watercress bunches, chop off base of stems to make short sprays. Crisp sprays in ice water for about 15 minutes, drain, and dry gently with paper towels. Place watercress around inside edge of lettuce. Sprinkle with sprouts, leaving center of plates clear.

Clean mushrooms and trim stems. Slice small mushrooms in half; larger ones into several slices. Add to plates around edges. Remove tops and points from baby carrots. Rinse and lightly scrape to clean. Slice in half lengthwise and arrange on salad, pointing out.

Shred turkey and mound in center of each plate. Sprinkle chopped almonds over all and dress with two to three tablespoons of vinaigrette.

YIELD: 6 SERVINGS

CHICKEN AND CRISPY GREENS

Turkey breasts are a natural substitute for the chicken in this recipe, combining well with the rich flavors of the dressing.

Dressing:

⅓ cup plain yogurt
2 tablespoons fresh chives, chopped
2 tablespoons fresh tarragon, chopped
1 clove garlic, minced
1 shallot, minced
2 tablespoons red wine vinegar

1 tablespoon dry sherry
½ cup walnut oil (or safflower oil)
2 tablespoons Dijon mustard
1 tablespoon cognac
Salt and freshly ground pepper, to taste

1½ pounds boneless, skinless chicken breasts
Salt and freshly ground pepper
2 tablespoons unsalted butter
1 teaspoon vegetable oil
3 cloves garlic, crushed
1 tablespoon dry sherry

2 heads Bibb lettuce
½ pound fresh spinach
6 ounces fresh green beans, trimmed and blanched
3 heads Belgian endive, trimmed and cored
2 tablespoons fresh chives, finely chopped
⅓ cup coarsely chopped walnuts

To prepare dressing, whisk together ingredients, blending well. Cover at room temperature until ready to use.

Pat the chicken breasts dry with paper towels and sprinkle both sides with salt and pepper. (Chicken should be near room temperature.) Melt butter and oil in a large skillet over medium-high heat. Add garlic and chicken breasts in one layer. Cook one minute, reduce heat to medium, and cook two more minutes. Discard garlic. Turn breasts over and cook until lightly browned and slightly pink inside. Add the sherry and cook until evaporated.

Slice chicken into julienne strips. Place in a bowl and pour on vinaigrette. Marinate for five minutes. On chilled salad plates, place lettuce leaves and spinach around perimeters and top with green beans and endive. Place chicken slices in middle and drizzle with vinaigrette, about two tablespoons per plate. (Serve reserve vinaigrette separately at table.) Sprinkle with chives and walnuts.

YIELD: 8 SERVINGS

CHICKEN AND BROCCOLI SALAD

The list of ingredients is long, but this salad is long on flavor. The chicken must be marinated in advance.

Chicken Marinade:

1 clove garlic, minced
1 teaspoon freshly grated ginger
1 teaspoon fresh cilantro, chopped
½ teaspoon crushed red chili peppers
2 tablespoons soy sauce
2 tablespoons sherry

2 whole boneless chicken breasts, skinned
3 tablespoons peanut oil

1 pound broccoli
1 sweet red pepper
1 yellow pepper

Vinaigrette:

2 tablespoons fresh lime juice
1 teaspoon freshly grated ginger
1 tablespoon cilantro, chopped
½ teaspoon brown sugar
Dash hot pepper sauce
½ teaspoon salt
½ teaspoon freshly ground pepper
2 tablespoons peanut oil
4 tablespoons safflower oil

¼ pound mushrooms, sliced
½ cup chopped scallions and tops

Combine marinade ingredients and blend well. Pound chicken breasts flat and coat with marinade. Cover and refrigerate at least 24 hours. Let stand at room temperature for 30 minutes before cooking. Pat chicken dry with paper towels. In a skillet, heat peanut oil until very hot. Place dry chicken in skillet and brown well, turning once, for a total cooking time of about five minutes. Remove from pan and drain. When cool, cut across grain into julienne slices. Chill.

Combine vinaigrette ingredients and mix well. Set aside. Cut florets from broccoli stalks. Peel stalks and slice on an angle into disks. Cook florets and disks in boiling salted water for about one to two minutes. Pour into a colander and douse immediately with cold water to stop cooking and retain color. Refrigerate.

Roast peppers under broiler or with long fork over flame until darkened on all sides. Place in a plastic bag in the freezer for 10 to 15 minutes. Remove skins and slice open to remove seeds and veins. Cut into julienne slices. Chill.

Before serving, place chicken, broccoli, peppers, mushrooms, and scallions in a large salad bowl. Add vinaigrette and toss.

YIELD: 4 TO 6 SERVINGS

ROQUEFORT CHICKEN SALAD

4 boneless chicken breasts
1 cup chicken broth
1 cup water
4 stalks celery
½ cup walnuts, very
   coarsely chopped
¼ pound Roquefort cheese,
   crumbled
2 tablespoons white
   wine vinegar
½ teaspoon Dijon mustard
Salt and freshly ground
   white pepper, to taste
6 tablespoons olive oil
2 heads Belgian endive
¼ teaspoon snipped fresh
   rosemary

Remove skin from chicken. In a large skillet, pour in one cup of water with the chicken broth. Bring to a boil, reduce heat, and add chicken breasts and celery. Poach gently for about five minutes. When done, chicken should be barely pink and the celery should be tender when pierced. Remove celery and rinse immediately with icy water to stop cooking process and retain color. Remove chicken to cool. Julienne both the chicken and celery and place in salad bowl. Sprinkle with walnuts and cheese.

In a separate bowl, combine vinegar, mustard, salt and pepper, and gradually whisk in olive oil until well blended. Pour over chicken mixture. Refrigerate if prepared ahead. Toss before serving.

Serve on chilled salad plates with leaves of endive. Sprinkle with rosemary to garnish.

YIELD: 6 TO 8 SERVINGS

WON TON CHICKEN SALAD

Dressing:

1 tablespoon sesame seeds
1 tablespoon sesame oil
¼ cup safflower oil
½ cup rice vinegar
1 tablespoon red wine
½ teaspoon salt
½ cup brown sugar
1 teaspoon hot chili oil

Peanut oil
6 ounces fresh won ton
  skins
3 whole cooked chicken
  breasts, skin and bones
  removed
1 bunch scallions
4 large stalks celery,
  julienned
1 small bunch cilantro,
  chopped
1 large head lettuce,
  shredded

To prepare dressing, combine sesame seeds and oils in a small skillet. Cook over medium heat, stirring constantly until the seeds are golden brown. Let cool slightly. Combine this mixture with the remaining dressing ingredients and blend well. Refrigerate.

Slice won tons into ¼-inch strips and deep fry in batches in approximately two inches of hot oil. Drain on paper towels. (Won tons can be stored in an air tight container at room temperature overnight.)

Shred chicken. Cut scallions into one-inch julienne strips. Combine chicken and scallions with celery, cilantro, and lettuce in a large bowl. Toss together. Add dressing and toss again. Salad can be refrigerated briefly at this point if necessary.

To serve, add won tons and toss gently. Do not let stand or won tons will lose their crispness.

YIELD: 8 SERVINGS

LAYERED CHICKEN SALAD

Fresh homemade mayonnaise cannot be praised enough for the difference it makes in salad dressings, especially creamy dressings for salads like this one. Our mayonnaise recipe appears in the margin.

Dressing:

1 cup mayonnaise
1 cup plain yogurt
1½ teaspoons curry powder
1 tablespoon sugar
½ teaspoon ground ginger

Salad:

4 cups shredded romaine
   lettuce
2 cups shredded nappa or
   Chinese cabbage
¼ pound bean sprouts
¾ cup water chestnuts,
   drained and sliced
¼ cup thinly sliced
   scallions
4 cups cooked skinless
   chicken breasts, shredded
1 cup fresh snow peas,
   trimmed and blanched
½ cup unsalted whole
   cashews

Prepare dressing by whisking together all ingredients. Cover and refrigerate overnight for flavors to blend.

Toss together shredded lettuce and cabbage. In a large salad bowl, layer salad ingredients, beginning with lettuce and cabbage on the bottom and follow with sprouts, water chestnuts, scallions, chicken, and snow peas. Pour dressing on top and spread to cover. Sprinkle with cashews.

YIELD: 8 TO 10 SERVINGS

For homemade mayonnaise, have the following ingredients at room temperature: 3 egg yolks, ½ teaspoon salt, 1 teaspoon prepared Dijon mustard, 1 tablespoon fresh lemon juice, 1 cup olive oil, salad oil, or a mixture of each, and freshly ground white pepper. Process yolks, salt, mustard, and lemon juice in a food processor with metal or plastic blade until yolks are pale yellow. While the machine is running, slowly dribble in oil through feed tube a few drops at a time at first, increasing slowly to a steady stream until all the oil is added. Taste and season with pepper. Cover and refrigerate. Makes one cup.

CHINESE CHICKEN AND WALNUT SALAD

The extra dressing this recipe makes can be used for similar salads. Consider substituting beef and toasted almonds or shrimp and toasted pine nuts for the chicken and walnuts.

Dressing:

1 cup corn oil
  (or walnut oil)
½ cup Hoisin sauce
½ cup soy sauce
½ cup red wine vinegar
1 tablespoon chopped
  garlic
1 tablespoon freshly grated
  ginger root
½ cup sesame seeds

Salad:

1 bunch spinach
½ bunch nappa or Chinese
  cabbage
4 carrots, julienned
1½ cups coarsely chopped
  walnuts
1 sweet red pepper, seeded
  and julienned
4 scallions, thinly sliced
2 cups cooked and
  shredded chicken

Combine dressing ingredients and blend well. Refrigerate. Wash spinach thoroughly and remove stems. Slice into ½-inch strips. Wash and core cabbage. Slice into ½-inch pieces. Dry and crisp in the refrigerator.

Combine greens and remaining salad ingredients in a large bowl. Toss well. Add dressing to taste and retoss. Reserve dressing may be stored in a covered glass container in the refrigerator.

YIELD: 6 TO 8 SERVINGS

SPICY CUCUMBER CHICKEN SALAD

3 whole boneless breasts of
  chicken
4 cucumbers, seeded and
  julienned

Dressing:

2 teaspoons Szechuan
  peppercorns
2 tablespoons sesame paste
  (or peanut butter)
1 tablespoon sugar
2 tablespoons white wine
  vinegar
4 tablespoons soy sauce,
  or more to taste
3 tablespoons minced
  scallions
3 tablespoons peeled and
  minced ginger root
2 tablespoons chopped
  garlic
2 tablespoons hot pepper
  oil

Broil chicken, turning once, until completely cooked but
still tender. Remove skin and chop into bitesize pieces.
Place cucumbers on serving plates and top with chicken.

Soften peppercorns in hot water. Drain and combine with
remaining dressing ingredients until well blended. Pour
dressing over chicken and serve.

Cucumber and chicken can be chilled in advance or
served at room temperature.

YIELD: 4 TO 6 SERVINGS

SHRIMP AND AVOCADO SALAD

¼ cup safflower oil
¼ cup white wine vinegar
3 large garlic cloves, minced
12 medium shrimp,
   cooked, peeled, and
   deveined
2 ripe avocados
Butter lettuce
2 tablespoons chopped
   blonde pistachios (salted)
Lemon slices (garnish)

Here's an excellent solution for what to do with too much of a good thing: When too many garlic cloves have been chopped for a recipe, the excess can be stored in olive oil in the refrigerator for a week or two, and the oil, now flavored, can also be used. Fresh basil leaves also keep this way, and excess chopped shallots will last several days in the refrigerator if stored in dry white wine.

Stir together oil, vinegar, and garlic. Cut four shrimp in half lengthwise and chop remaining shrimp into half-inch pieces. Add shrimp to oil mixture. Cut avocados in half lengthwise and remove pits. With a teaspoon, scoop out a few bitesize chunks from the pit area and add to shrimp mixture. With a tablespoon, carefully scoop entire avocado half from skin in one piece.

Place each avocado on lettuce leaves on a chilled salad plate. Remove shrimp halves from oil mixture and set aside. Fill avocados with remaining shrimp mixture. Top each with two shrimp halves and sprinkle with pistachios. Garnish salad plates with lemon slices and serve immediately.

YIELD: 4 SERVINGS

MARINATED ARTICHOKE AND SHRIMP SALAD

Marinade:

⅔ cup white wine vinegar
1 teaspoon salt
¼ teaspoon freshly ground
  pepper
¼ teaspoon dried oregano
Dash paprika
Dash cayenne
1 bay leaf, crumbled
1 clove garlic, minced
1⅓ cups olive oil

Salad:

6 artichokes
Rind and juice of ½ lemon
½ pound shrimp
2 ripe tomatoes, sliced
2 avocados, peeled and
  sliced

Whisk together marinade ingredients, adding oil gradually until well blended.

Cook artichokes 30 to 40 minutes or until tender in boiling water with lemon rind. Pierce stems to check. When done, drain and rinse with cold water. Discard all inedible outside leaves and trim ends of stems. Remove firm outer leaves and place in a bowl. Drizzle with lemon juice. Remove hearts and chop, along with stems, into large pieces. Add to bowl. Reserve ½ cup of marinade and pour remainder over artichokes. Toss to coat all pieces. Cover and refrigerate several hours or overnight.

Cook shrimp in boiling water until done. Drain and douse immediately in cold water. Peel and devein. Chop into large pieces. When cooled, place in a bowl and pour in reserve marinade. Toss to coat all pieces. Cover.

To serve, remove artichoke leaves from marinade and place in petal fashion on individual salad plates. Place tomato slices in center and top with avocado slices. Add artichoke hearts and stems and top with shrimp. Drizzle with marinade.

YIELD: 6 SERVINGS

Some cooks prefer to leave shells on when boiling shrimp for salads. Others remove the shells first so that shrimp can be deveined before cooking. Shrimp may stay more moist if cooked in shells, and they don't curl up as much. On the other hand, if veins are thick, removing them first may avoid an unwanted flavor. Either way. It's just one of the many decisions cooks make—decisions that make good cooks.

SPICY SHRIMP SALAD

This salad has a "hot" flavor whether warm or chilled. As a first course for a Mexican menu, serve warm with Mexican spoon bread (see page 41). For a cold salad, serve with crusty French bread or with avocado slices and warm tortilla chips.

Vinaigrette:

⅓ cup olive oil
5 tablespoons fresh lime
   juice
Salt and freshly ground
   pepper, to taste
Dash cayenne or dash
   Tabasco
2 tablespoons fresh
   cilantro, chopped

Salad:

1 cup jicama, peeled and
   julienned
2 tablespoons peanut oil
2 red chili peppers
2 shallots, chopped
2 pounds shrimp, peeled
   and deveined
¼ cup scallions,
   sliced very thin

Jicama, a tuber, is a member of the morning glory family and is added to salads for its crisp, almost sweet flavor. When cooked, jicama doesn't lose its crunchy texture, making it a good substitute for water chestnuts in stir-fry dishes. Select small, young tubers that are solid and unblemished—these are more tender and tasty. Peel the brown skin just before serving. Unpeeled jicama will keep over a week if chilled. Peak season is from August to October.

Prepare vinaigrette by mixing ingredients thoroughly. Pour about a fourth of the vinaigrette over jicama and set aside.

Heat peanut oil in a large skillet, break chilies in half and add to oil. Add shallots first, then shrimp, being careful not to cool the oil. Cook for about one minute, stirring and turning shrimp. Do not overcook. Remove from pan and discard chilies. Toss shrimp and shallots immediately in the vinaigrette. Add jicama and scallions and serve at once.

To serve chilled, prepare vinaigrette and refrigerate. Cook shrimp and shallots as indicated but allow to cool. Add to vinaigrette and chill. Before serving, slice jicama and scallions, add to mixture and serve on leaf lettuce.

YIELD: 6 SERVINGS

SHRIMP REMOULADE

Remoulade:

2 cloves garlic, minced
⅓ cup horseradish mustard
2 tablespoons catsup
2½ tablespoons paprika
¾ teaspoon cayenne
½ teaspoon salt
⅓ cup white wine vinegar
½ cup olive oil
½ cup finely chopped
  scallions, including tops

Salad:

1 pound large fresh shrimp
Bibb lettuce
Fresh dill sprigs (garnish)

Combine remoulade ingredients in a large bowl and whisk until well blended.

Cook shrimp in boiling water until done. Immediately douse in cold water to stop cooking process. Repeat as needed until shrimp are thoroughly cooled. Drain thoroughly, peel and devein. Add shrimp to remoulade, tossing to coat pieces. Cover bowl and marinate for several hours in refrigerator.

Wash lettuce thoroughly and place leaves on serving plates. Top leaves with marinated shrimp and garnish with dill.

YIELD: 4 TO 6 SERVINGS

Instead of using only salted water for boiling shrimp, consider this suggestion. For one pound of shrimp, combine the following in a four-quart saucepan: 2 cups water, ¼ cup or more white wine, onion slices, chopped celery, a bay leaf, parsley sprigs, a teaspoon of whole pepper-corns, and a few slices of fresh lemon. Bring to a boil, cover, reduce heat and simmer for five minutes. Add shrimp, bring to a boil un-covered, remove pan from heat, cover, and let stand a few minutes. Drain.

SHRIMP AND VEGETABLES IN HERB VINAIGRETTE

The vegetables and shrimp should be marinated overnight.

Vinaigrette:

⅓ cup white wine vinegar
1 tablespoon Dijon mustard
2 tablespoons chopped
  fresh Italian parsley
2 tablespoons chopped
  fresh tarragon
2 tablespoons chopped
  chives
½ teaspoon dried chervil
½ teaspoon capers
3 black olives, minced
1 cup olive oil
1 teaspoon freshly ground
  pepper

Salad:

1 pound fresh shrimp
½ head cauliflower
½ pound broccoli
1 green pepper
1 sweet red pepper
1 red onion
½ pound fresh mushrooms
Romaine lettuce
Full sprigs of Italian
  parsley (garnish)

Like many herbs, chervil was once thought to have medicinal properties—good for eye problems, bruises, or even the hiccups. The Greeks called it the "leaf of joy." A delicate herb, it's ideal for delicate dishes, such as salads with mild greens, chicken, fish, or light soups. Chervil adds tang; it has a sweet, aniselike flavor. Combined with a touch of tarragon, it makes an excellent herb butter for bass, snapper, lobster, halibut, or monkfish. Fresh chervil substitutes well for parsley.

To prepare vinaigrette, combine vinegar, mustard, herbs, and seasonings in a large bowl and let stand ten minutes. Add oil gradually, whisking well. Cover and refrigerate.

Cook shrimp in boiling water until done. Drain and immediately douse in cold water until thoroughly cooled, repeating if necessary. Peel and devein.

Remove stems from cauliflower and broccoli and chop florets into bitesize pieces. Remove stem, seeds, and veins from peppers and slice. Peel and thinly slice the onion. Rinse mushrooms and wipe dry. Trim stems and slice. Combine vegetables and shrimp with vinaigrette, tossing well to cover all pieces. Marinate overnight.

Place washed leaves of romaine on chilled salad plates. Add marinated salad and garnish with parsley sprigs.

YIELD: 6 TO 8 SERVINGS

CALIFORNIA SHRIMP RING

2 pounds fresh shrimp
Juice of 1 lemon
1 envelope unflavored
  gelatin
2 tablespoons water
⅓ cup fresh lemon juice
4 cups cream cheese
¾ teaspoon sugar
2 tablespoons chopped
  Italian parsley
1 teaspoon grated lemon
  peel
½ teaspoon salt
¼ teaspoon freshly ground
  pepper
10 ounces plum preserves
3 tablespoons Pickapeppa
  sauce
1 head green-leaf lettuce
1 lemon, thinly sliced
Sprigs of Italian parsley

Cook shrimp in boiling water until done. Douse immediately in cold water. Drain, peel, and devein. Chop half the shrimp into small pieces and set aside. Place remaining whole shrimp in a bowl and squeeze lemon juice over all pieces and toss. Cover bowl and set aside in a cool place.

Combine gelatin, water, and lemon juice in a saucepan. Stir over low heat until gelatin is dissolved. Remove from heat.

Beat together cream cheese, sugar, parsley, lemon peel, salt, and pepper in a large bowl. (This is easier if cream cheese is soft at room temperature.) Blend in gelatin mixture and fold in chopped shrimp by hand. Pour into a 6½ cup ring mold and chill to firm.

To serve: Layer lettuce on a serving plate and unmold salad on top. Combine plum preserves and pickapeppa sauce. Drizzle over mold. Garnish lettuce with lemon slices, and parsley sprigs, and fill center of mold with whole shrimp.

YIELD: 20 TO 24 SERVINGS

Green-leaf lettuce, or salad bowl lettuce, was developed in California. Along with the similar red-leaf and romaine, it is available most of the year. Leaves should be torn for salads rather than cut with a knife, which tends to discolor edges.

CRAB SALAD

This versatile salad is ideal for substituting other ingredients as desired. Smoked fish, Japanese-style raw fish, calamari strips, or shrimp are all excellent alternatives to crabmeat.

1 teaspoon lemon juice
Dash paprika
Dash Worcestershire sauce
1 teaspoon horseradish
4 cups cooked crabmeat

Vinaigrette:

3 tablespoons red wine
   vinegar
2 tablespoons Dijon
   mustard
1 clove garlic, minced
2 black olives, minced
Freshly ground pepper,
   to taste
½ cup olive oil

Salad:

6 ripe tomatoes, sliced
6 hearts of palm, chunked
4 avocados, peeled and
   sliced
2 pink grapefruits, peeled
   and sectioned
½ cup black olives

Combine lemon juice, paprika, Worcestershire sauce, and horseradish in a bowl and whisk together. Add crabmeat and toss to cover all pieces. Cover and refrigerate one to two hours.

To prepare vinaigrette, whisk together vinegar, mustard, garlic, olives, and pepper, and gradually whisk in oil until well blended. Refrigerate.

On a large serving platter, arrange tomato slices in two layers around the edge. Distribute hearts of palm around inside of tomatoes, followed by avocados, then grapefruit. Mound crabmeat in the center and garnish the platter with olives. Drizzle vinaigrette to taste over entire platter.

YIELD: 6 TO 8 SERVINGS

MEDITERRANEAN SALAD

Vinaigrette:

5 tablespoons freshly
  squeezed lemon juice
2 cloves garlic, minced
2 teaspoons fresh thyme
2 teaspoons summer savory
½ teaspoon salt
½ teaspoon freshly ground
  pepper
10 tablespoons olive oil

Salad:

1 medium eggplant
1 pound shrimp
¼ pound feta cheese,
  crumbled
1 cup Greek olives
1 head romaine lettuce
2 ripe tomatoes, peeled
⅓ cup chopped parsley
  (garnish)

Whisk together all vinaigrette ingredients. Refrigerate.

Peel and julienne eggplant. Salt and let drain in a colander for 30 minutes. Cook shrimp in boiling water. Drain and douse immediately in cold water to stop cooking process. Peel and devein. In a large bowl, pour half the vinaigrette over the shrimp, tossing to cover. Add feta cheese and toss again. Refrigerate. Rinse the eggplant and drain well. Pour on the remaining vinaigrette. Add olives and toss well. Refrigerate.

Just before serving, toss together the shrimp and eggplant mixtures. Cut tomatoes into wedges. Serve on leaves of romaine and surround with tomatoes. Garnish with parsley.

YIELD: 4 SERVINGS

PACIFIC SUNSET SALAD

Dressing:

½ cup mayonnaise
½ cup plain yogurt
½ cup sour cream
3 tablespoons freshly
   squeezed lemon juice
½ teaspoon dry mustard
½ clove garlic, minced
1 teaspoon curry powder
Salt, to taste

Salad:

1 pound pork roast
   (or 1 pound fresh shrimp)
¼ cup soy sauce
½ clove garlic, minced
2 bunches spinach
12 slices fresh pineapple
2 whole papayas, pared
   and sliced
8 ounces macadamia nuts,
   chopped

Prepare dressing by blending together all ingredients. Refrigerate at least one to two hours before serving.

Cut pork into thin strips. Mix soy sauce and garlic and pour over pork, covering all pieces. Marinate at room temperature 30 minutes. Pour off marinade and cook pork strips under broiler until done, about three minutes each side. Remove and drain on paper towels. When cool, cut into bitesize pieces. Refrigerate. (If shrimp is substituted, remove shells, clean shrimp, and marinate. Broil, being careful not to overcook. Cut into pieces and refrigerate.)

Wash spinach thoroughly. Remove stems and damaged leaves. Dry thoroughly. Place leaves on chilled salad plates and top with pineapple and papaya slices, follow with pork, and sprinkle on nuts. Add dressing just before serving.

YIELD: 4 SERVINGS

SUPERB CREAMY VINAIGRETTE

Excellent as a marinade for raw or cooked vegetables or as a spicy dressing for mixed greens.

½ cup olive oil
½ cup plain yogurt
½ cup cream
2 cloves garlic, minced
⅓ cup tarragon vinegar
1 raw egg
1 tablespoon salt

1½ teaspoons freshly
  ground black pepper
1 tablespoon sugar
1 teaspoon dry mustard
1 tablespoon Dijon mustard
3 tablespoons freshly grated
  Parmesan cheese

Combine all ingredients and blend well (or shake in jar) until smooth. Cover and refrigerate.

YIELD: APPROXIMATELY 2 CUPS

WHOLE GRAIN MUSTARD VINAIGRETTE

Delicious with green salads, steamed eggplant, or antipasto.

1 tablespoon whole grain
  mustard
2 cloves garlic, peeled
2 tablespoons red wine
  vinegar
½ teaspoon freshly ground
  pepper
1 teaspoon salt
½ cup olive oil
5 to 6 basil leaves

Place all ingredients in food processor or blender and mix well. Transfer to a covered nonmetal container and refrigerate. Reblend by hand before serving.

YIELD: FOR A SALAD THAT SERVES 4 TO 6

Salt is included in many vinaigrettes, and for these and other uncooked dressings, kosher salt is ideal. Kosher salt is iodized and has more flavor than "table" salt, making it possible to use smaller quantities. Even though the difference in taste is not great, some discerning palates can detect it. Adding salt "to taste" is always a good idea.

TONI'S FAVORITE VINAIGRETTE

This delicious salad dressing from Antonia Allegra, Food Editor of the *San Diego Tribune* also works wonderfully as a marinade for barbecued chicken or fish and as a base for an onion-lentil salad.

2 tablespoons Balsamic
  vinegar
6 tablespoons olive oil
2 to 3 cloves garlic, finely
  chopped
1 teaspoon Dijon mustard
1 tablespoon stone ground
  mustard (Moutarde de
  Meaux preferred)

Combine all ingredients, stirring with fork or whisk until an emulsion is formed. If stored in the refrigerator, rewhisk before using.

YIELD: APPROXIMATELY ONE CUP

BALSAMIC VINEGAR SALAD DRESSING

Bill Waite, Hospitality Director for Dennis Conner and Sail America at the America's Cup Races, sends us his heretofore secret dressing recipe. Bill calls it "Sonoma Gold." He tosses the leaves of two heads of crisped butterleaf or Boston lettuce in the dressing, making enough salad for four servings.

2 cloves garlic, minced
⅓ to ½ cup extra-virgin
  olive oil
2 tablespoons walnut or
  hazelnut oil (optional)
1 egg yolk
1 heaping tablespoon Dijon
  mustard
1 teaspoon freshly squeezed
  lime juice
2 tablespoons Balsamic
  vinegar (Aceto "Fini"
  Gold Label preferred)

Rub garlic into the bottom and sides of a wooden salad bowl until oil of the garlic is extracted. Remove excess garlic fibers. Pour olive and walnut oils into bowl. Add egg yolk, mustard, lime juice, and vinegar. Whisk together, collecting garlic oil from sides of the bowl, until a creamy texture is obtained.

YIELD: 4 SERVINGS

The best olive oils are cold-pressed and come from the first pressing of hand-picked olives. These oils are superior in flavor, aroma, and nutrient content. The least acidic oils with the mellowest taste are labeled "extra-virgin," and are ideal in salad dressings. Store olive oil in a glass container in a cool, dark place.

BLUE CHEESE DRESSING

5 ounces blue cheese
(Gorgonzola or
Roquefort)
1 cup mayonnaise
(homemade preferred)
½ cup plain yogurt
1 cup sour cream
1 garlic clove, minced

¼ teaspoon freshly ground
pepper
½ teaspoon white wine
vinegar
1 teaspoon Worcestershire
sauce
½ teaspoon salt

Set aside half the cheese. Prepare mayonnaise (see recipe on page 134) and combine with all other ingredients. Blend well until smooth. Crumble reserve cheese and add to dressing. Cover and refrigerate.

YIELD: APPROXIMATELY 3 CUPS

Garlic yields several distinct flavors depending on how it is prepared. The more a garlic clove is sliced, the more aromatic oils are released. For vinaigrettes or marinades, whole peeled cloves can be added to the oil and seasonings and left overnight, resulting in a mild garlicky flavor instead of an acrid one. For a stronger taste or for short-term marinades, halve a clove, remove the bitter green sprout in the center, and chop. The less aggressive you are with the knife, the less intense that infamous garlic aftertaste will be.

GARLIC DRESSING

Excellent for green salads made with crisp romaine lettuce or as a marinade for grilled or baked chicken, fish, lamb, or kebabs.

1½ cups safflower oil
½ cup fresh lemon juice
1½ teaspoons salt
1 teaspoon coarsely ground
pepper

10 drops Tabasco
6 cloves garlic, peeled and
crushed
1 cup freshly grated
Parmesan cheese

Whisk together all ingredients or combine in a large jar and shake well. Refrigerate at least eight hours or overnight for flavors to blend. Dressing will keep in the refrigerator up to one week. Rewhisk before using.

YIELD: APPROXIMATELY 3 CUPS

Marvelous Complements

Marvelous Complements

VEGETABLES, RICE, PASTA

Side dishes California Style. That's a decided contradiction in terms. The saucy audacity of pasta recipes, the unmistakable crunch of fresh vegetables, and the versatility of rice dishes refuse sideline treatment. Other courses are complemented by the preparations in this section, but many of these marvelous dishes easily withstand undivided attention. They are inventive, full of freshness, and celebrate California's vast selection of homegrown foods.

The way California cooking assimilates ethnic influences is strongly featured here. Hot and Sour Zucchini, Vegetable Burritos, and Pasta Primavera with Marinara Sauce are a sampling of the many recipes that reflect the rich heritage other cultures have contributed to the table. Szechuan peppercorns, Ortega chilies, artichokes, or cilantro may be exotic fare elsewhere, but these and other unusual ingredients are familiar to us. Combined with what seems an endless abundance of California-grown produce and a little inspiration, these ingredients give vegetables, rice, and pasta dishes a character all their own, a California style.

ASPARAGUS MOUSSE WITH ORANGE SAUCE

The mousse mixture may fill more than the six ramekins called for. All the better for the cook, who may be tempted to preview this delicious dish when it comes out of the oven.

Mousse:

1 pound fresh early
  asparagus
1½ cups heavy cream
3 eggs
2 egg yolks
¾ teaspoon salt
¼ teaspoon freshly ground
  black pepper
Grated nutmeg, to taste

Sauce:

¼ teaspoon salt
Peel of 1 medium orange
1 clove garlic
4 shallots
½ cup dry white wine
1¼ cups freshly squeezed
  orange juice
1 teaspoon cider vinegar
2 teaspoons orange liqueur
¾ cup unsalted butter,
  melted
6 orange slices, peeled and
  seeds removed (garnish)

Once you've snapped off the tough ends from asparagus and peeled the skins from mature spears, either steam the asparagus or lay it in a skillet, cover with cold water, add a pinch of salt, and boil, uncovered, about six minutes or so. Remove one spear with tongs and shake it gently; if the head bobs, the asparagus is done.

Remove and discard tough ends from asparagus stalks. Steam stalks about 10 minutes or until tender. Puree in blender or food processor. Add cream, blend, and strain to remove fiber. In a bowl, add eggs, yolks, salt, pepper, and nutmeg to puree. Stir well to combine. Divide mixture evenly among six buttered ramekins or custard cups. Place ramekins in a one-inch water bath in a baking pan. Bake about 20 to 25 minutes or until a knife inserted in the center is withdrawn clean. Keep warm in water bath until serving time.

To prepare sauce, combine salt and orange peel in blender or processor. Process until peel is chopped. Add garlic and shallots. Mince. Place mixture in a non-aluminum saucepan. Add wine and orange juice. Simmer and reduce to a half cup when strained. Return to processor (cleaned) and add vinegar and liqueur. With machine running, add butter. Process five seconds.

To serve, spoon three to four tablespoons sauce on warm serving plates. Loosen each mousse with knife and unmold in center of plate. Garnish with orange slices and serve immediately.

YIELD: 6 SERVINGS

SPUNKY ASPARAGUS

An easy, sweet and sour dish that should be prepared a day ahead and served slightly chilled.

**3 pounds fresh early
  asparagus**
⅔ cup white vinegar
½ cup sugar
½ teaspoon salt
1 teaspoon whole cloves
3 sticks cinnamon
1 tablespoon celery seed
½ cup water
**Orange zest or grated
  hard-cooked egg (garnish)**

Snap tough ends from asparagus stalks and discard. Steam or cook spears until just tender. Douse immediately in cold water. Drain. Place asparagus in the bottom of a baking dish.

Bring vinegar, sugar, salt, spices, and water to a boil in a saucepan. Pour hot liquid over asparagus. Cover and allow to cool. Refrigerate overnight or up to 24 hours.

To serve, pour off liquid, place asparagus on serving plates, and garnish with orange zest or egg.

YIELD: 6 SERVINGS

Peanut oil will help retain the fresh, green color of vegetables when they are cooked. Add a tablespoon of oil to about two to three quarts of water. When steaming vegetables, cover pot only partially and vegetables will keep their brilliant color.

CHILLED DILLED PEAS

A refreshing side dish that doubles and triples easily.

1 cup sour cream
1 bunch fresh chives,
    snipped
¼ cup fresh snipped dill
1 teaspoon curry powder,
    or to taste
Salt and freshly ground
    pepper, to taste
1 pound frozen petite peas,
    uncooked and thawed

Many of us have gotten into the habit of placing side dishes alongside the entree on the same plate and not actually in a side dish. For different presentation, use small dishes (they don't have to match) for side dishes at each setting.

Combine sour cream, chives, dill, curry powder, salt and pepper. Add peas and gently mix. Chill thoroughly a few hours or overnight. Garnish with freshly snipped dill. Serve cold.

YIELD: 4 TO 6 SERVINGS

SESAME BROCCOLI

1 large bunch broccoli
⅔ cup sesame seeds,
    toasted
¼ cup sake
2 tablespoons soy sauce
2 teaspoons sesame oil
2 teaspoons honey
Dash Tabasco

Vegetables can be partially cooked ahead of time, doused in ice water, and quickly sauteed to reheat before serving. This prevents soggy or overcooked vegetables.

Trim florets and small stems from broccoli. Discard main stem. Cook broccoli in boiling salted water until crisp-tender. Douse in cold water, drain thoroughly, and let stand until cooled to room temperature. Combine remaining ingredients in a large bowl. Add broccoli and toss to cover all pieces.

YIELD: 6 SERVINGS

BAKED BROCCOLI AND ONIONS

1 pound fresh broccoli
2 cups pearl onions (or 3
   medium onions, quartered)
¼ cup unsalted butter
2 tablespoons flour
¼ teaspoon salt
Freshly ground pepper,
   to taste

1 cup milk
3 ounces cream cheese,
   softened
½ cup shredded sharp
   Cheddar cheese
1 cup bread crumbs
¼ teaspoon thyme

Preheat oven to 350 degrees. Cut up broccoli, small stems and florets, and steam until just tender. Drain and set aside. Peel onions and cook in boiling salted water until tender. Drain and set aside.

Melt two tablespoons butter in a one-quart saucepan, blend in flour, salt, and pepper. Add milk and stir mixture constantly until thick and bubbly. Do not boil. Reduce heat and blend in cream cheese until smooth.

Place broccoli and onions in the bottom of a buttered casserole dish (1½-quart capacity). Pour sauce over the top and toss gently. Top with cheese.

Melt remaining butter and stir in bread crumbs and thyme. Sprinkle over casserole and bake uncovered 40 to 45 minutes.

YIELD: 6 SERVINGS

The ancient Egyptians supposedly worshipped onions. They can add divine flavors to many dishes, but can be rapscallions to peel—especially small or pearl onions. This peeling technique works well: Let onions simmer in boiling water a few minutes. Drain and cool. The peels are then easily pulled off.

BROCCOLI FLAN

1 bunch broccoli
1 cup milk
1 cup cream
3 eggs
3 egg yolks
¼ teaspoon grated nutmeg
¼ teaspoon salt
Freshly ground white
  pepper, to taste
¼ cup chopped pecans

2 tablespoons butter
6 shallots, chopped
½ pound mushrooms,
  thinly sliced
½ cup mixed fresh herbs,
  finely chopped (parsley,
  chervil, chives, basil,
  for example)

Preheat oven to 350 degrees. Butter eight small souffle
dishes or ramekins and line the bottom of each with
waxed paper. Set dishes in a large baking pan at least two
inches deep.

Remove large stems from broccoli and break up florets.
Add florets to boiling salted water and cook two minutes.
Drain, then douse in cold water. Set aside in a colander.

Whisk together milk, cream, eggs, nutmeg, salt and pepper.
To the bottom of each souffle dish, add broccoli and
pecans, and pour milk mixture on top. Add hot water to
the baking pan holding souffle dishes and place in oven.
Cook 20 to 30 minutes. Remove from oven.

Melt butter in a skillet, add shallots and saute until tender.
Add mushrooms and saute one minute. Remove from heat.
Unmold each flan, spoon mushrooms over each, and
garnish with herbs.

YIELD: 8 SERVINGS

RATATOUILLE NICOISE

Zucchini and eggplant are available most of the time, so this dish can be prepared any season. Serve chilled on warm weather days or warm from the pot on nippy evenings. Can be prepared in advance and refrigerated to blend flavors fully.

2 zucchini, sliced
1 eggplant, peeled and
    cubed
3 tablespoons flour
⅓ cup olive oil
2 cloves garlic, minced
1 red onion, sliced
2 green peppers, seeded and
    cut into large strips
5 ripe tomatoes, peeled and
    chunked
Salt and freshly ground
    pepper, to taste
1 tablespoon capers

Toss zucchini and eggplant in flour. Set aside. Heat oil in a heavy four-quart pot. Add garlic and onion and saute until tender. Add zucchini and eggplant along with green peppers. Cover pot and cook slowly over low heat for one hour. Add tomatoes and simmer uncovered until mixture thickens. Add salt and pepper. During the last 15 minutes of cooking, add capers.

YIELD: 6 TO 8 SERVINGS

"A la nicoise" is a way of preparing a dish, usually flavored with garlic, in which tomatoes are a featured ingredient.

ZUCCHINI AND EGGPLANT ALMONDINE

Grilled fish couldn't have better company.

1 cup slivered almonds
¼ pound bacon, cut up
1 pound zucchini, sliced
1 pound eggplant, diced
1 large onion, cut into
    wedges
1 tablespoon flour
1 pound ripe tomatoes,
    cooked and chopped
1 clove garlic, minced
1 teaspoon salt
¼ teaspoon freshly ground
    pepper
2 tablespoons chopped
    fresh basil
6 ounces Swiss cheese,
    sliced

Beautiful, unusual eggplant, with its dark, patent skin, is a versatile and much over-looked vegetable. It combines well with strong seasonings and mixes well with other vegetables. Eggplants usually don't need peeling, especially if they're small and young. The peel should be glossy and smooth. Buy them firm and use within a day or two. Be frugal with oil or butter with this vegetable—the pulp is very absorbent. Salting after chopping or slicing helps and also leaches some of the juice, which can be bitter.

Preheat oven to 400 degrees. Saute almonds with bacon until bacon is crisp. Remove from skillet and set aside. Add zucchini, eggplant, and onion to skillet, cover and cook 15 minutes over low heat. Mix in flour, tomatoes, garlic, salt, pepper, and basil.

In the bottom of a buttered two-quart baking dish, place a layer of vegetables, top with cheese, followed by nuts and bacon mixture. Repeat layers ending with nuts and bacon. (Can be refrigerated at this point for advance preparation. Bring to room temperature before baking.)

Bake uncovered 30 minutes.

YIELD: 8 TO 10 SERVINGS

ZUCCHINI WITH PESTO

Pesto:

¼ cup freshly grated
  Parmesan cheese
¼ cup olive oil
3 tablespoons coarsely
  chopped fresh basil
1 clove garlic

Saltato:

2 tablespoons olive oil
3 medium zucchini, cubed
1 small onion, minced
3 medium tomatoes, cubed
1 teaspoon salt

Combine pesto ingredients in a blender or food processor and blend until smooth.

Place a large skillet over high heat until very hot. Add oil, coating bottom evenly. Stir fry zucchini in oil three minutes. Add onion, stirring constantly another three minutes. Add tomatoes and salt and stir fry one minute. Remove from heat, add pesto, and stir briskly until thoroughly mixed. Serve immediately.

YIELD: 4 SERVINGS

Southern California's sunny seasons give us fresh basil year-round. The heady flavor of basil blends beautifully with dishes of any season— from summer's ripest tomatoes to winter's savory stews. As a garnish for a simple vegetable side dish, add basil to steamed zucchini, sauteed eggplant, or to rice with slices of roasted sweet peppers.

HOT AND SOUR ZUCCHINI

A quick, stir fry vegetable truly enlivened by ginger root and red pepper.

1 pound zucchini
4 teaspoons chopped ginger
  root
4 teaspoons chopped garlic
  cloves
4 teaspoons finely chopped
  scallions
3 teaspoons cornstarch
½ cup vinegar
2½ tablespoons soy sauce
¼ cup sugar
⅓ cup vegetable oil
4 teaspoons sesame oil
4 dried red peppers
2 teaspoons Szechuan
  peppercorns

Wash zucchini and slice into quarter-inch rounds. Place zucchini in a bowl with ginger, garlic, and scallions. In a separate bowl, combine cornstarch, vinegar, soy sauce, and sugar.

Heat oil in a wok until hot, being careful not to burn. Add red peppers and peppercorns. Stir fry 15 seconds.

Add zucchini mixture, tossing to coat. Stir fry one minute. Add cornstarch mixture and toss to coat. Allow sauce to thicken. Serve immediately.

YIELD: 4 SERVINGS

BAKED ZUCCHINI WITH MOZZARELLA CHEESE

1½ pounds fresh zucchini
4 eggs
½ cup milk
1 pound freshly grated
  mozzarella cheese
1 teaspoon salt
2 teaspoons baking powder
3 tablespoons flour
½ cup bread crumbs
3 tablespoons butter,
  or less to taste

Preheat oven to 350 degrees. Wash and cut zucchini in half-inch slices. Steam or cook until slightly tender but still firm. Drain and douse in cold water. Drain again and set aside.

Beat eggs lightly. Add milk, cheese, salt, baking powder, and flour. Stir in zucchini. Place mixture in a buttered baking dish (9 x 13 inches), sprinkle with bread crumbs, and dot with butter. Bake uncovered 35 to 40 minutes.

YIELD: 6 SERVINGS

ACORN SQUASH RAVIOLI WITH CREAM AND MARJORAM

Jack Huxtable, chef at Sheppard's Restaurant in San Diego, contributes this creative recipe. The distinctive flavor of squash is enhanced by a touch of nutmeg and beautifully complemented by fresh marjoram.

½ acorn squash
Salt, freshly ground pepper,
   to taste
1 package won ton skins
1 small onion, diced
1 ounce butter
1 cup chicken broth
2 cups heavy cream
1 bunch fresh marjoram

An acorn squash averages about one to three pounds and gets its name from its acorn shape—and probably from the nutty flavor as well. The squash is pleated, has a dark green skin that is sometimes mottled with orange, and has a lush, peach-colored flesh. Although available year-round, acorn squash peak in cooler months.

Remove seeds from squash and peel with a sharp knife. Cut into one-inch pieces. Cook in boiling salted water until done, about 20 minutes. Drain very well. Puree in a food processor or blender and season to taste.

Place small portions of the puree in the center of each won ton skin. Moisten the edges with water, fold and seal with fingertips. Set aside.

Saute onion in butter, add chicken broth, and cook to reduce liquid by two-thirds. Add cream. Chop half of the marjoram and add. Reduce sauce by half. Strain and season with salt and pepper if desired. Keep sauce warm. Remove stems from remaining marjoram and set aside for garnish.

Cook ravioli in boiling, salted water for about five minutes. Drain and mix with cream sauce. Garnish with marjoram.

YIELD: 4 SERVINGS

CABBAGE WITH APPLES AND WALNUTS

6 slices bacon
⅓ cup apple cider vinegar
½ cup water
½ cup brown sugar
½ medium red cabbage, shredded
½ medium green cabbage, shredded
2 crisp apples, thinly sliced (Jonathan or Winesap preferred)
⅓ cup chopped walnuts, toasted

In a large skillet, cook bacon until very crisp. Remove bacon and drain on paper towels. Crumble and set aside. Pour off all but three tablespoons of bacon fat in skillet. Add vinegar, water, and brown sugar. Cook until reduced by one third.

Add cabbage and cook, tossing constantly, until it wilts. Toss in apples. Serve warm with walnuts and crumbled bacon on top.

YIELD: 6 TO 8 SERVINGS

Apart from the loss of nutrients, one reason not to overcook members of the cabbage family, which includes cauliflower, broccoli, Brussels sprouts, and others in addition to cabbage—is that the longer these vegetables are cooked, the more hydrogen sulfide is produced, that irritating odor and flavor that only gains in potency with cooking time.

CARROTS WITH PISTACHIOS AND COINTREAU

**5 tablespoons unsalted
  butter**
**½ cup shelled, blonde
  pistachios**
¼ cup Cointreau
**1 pound carrots, cut on
  diagonal into ¼-inch
  slices**
3 tablespoons water
1 teaspoon salt

*Back in the old days, carrots
were purple or red, even
black. In the 1600s, in
Holland, a paler carrot was
developed, the type we know
today. Carrots are not native
to this continent; they were
brought here by the colonists.
Queen Ann's Lace, the wild-
flower, is actually the carrot
the colonists brought, but it
escaped cultivation to become
wild.*

Melt two tablespoons butter over medium-high heat.
Add pistachios and saute one minute. Stir in Cointreau,
remove from heat, and set aside.

Combine carrots, remaining butter, water, and salt in a large
saucepan. Bring to a boil, reduce heat, cover and cook
until carrots are crisp-tender, about five minutes. Use a
slotted spoon to transfer carrots to heated serving dish.
Keep warm. Boil cooking liquid until reduced to two tablespoons. Add to pistachio mixture and pour over carrots.
Serve immediately.

YIELD: 6 SERVINGS

BAKED ARTICHOKE HEARTS AND MUSHROOMS

An excellent side dish for roast beef, grilled beef or pork, or grilled seafood. Marinated artichoke hearts do not substitute for this recipe. Look for frozen hearts if fresh artichokes aren't at their best.

2 cups cooked artichoke
   hearts, quartered
½ cup freshly grated
   Parmesan cheese
2 tablespoons unsalted
   butter
½ pound fresh mushrooms,
   sliced
1 cup heavy cream
½ teaspoon chervil
3 tablespoons dry sherry
   (optional)

Preheat oven to 350 degrees. Arrange artichokes in a buttered baking dish (1½-quart capacity). Sprinkle with half the cheese.

Melt butter and saute mushrooms until tender. Add cream and cook over low heat, stirring occasionally, until most of the cream is absorbed. Do not boil. Stir in chervil and sherry. Pour mixture over the artichokes and sprinkle with remaining cheese. Bake 20 to 30 minutes.

YIELD: 4 TO 6 SERVINGS

To prepare fresh artichoke hearts, snap off outer leaves until leaves with pale bases are evident. Snip off dark tops of outer pale leaves. Peel dark covering from stem and pare the stem toward the leaves. Cut off the base of the stem. Slice artichokes into wedges and remove the fuzzy chokes with a paring knife. Boil in a large pot of water with one teaspoon of salt added per quart, and with lemon juice or lemon rind added also. Cook until just tender, about ten minutes. Pierce heart with a fork to test tenderness.

CARAWAY POTATOES WITH SWISS CHEESE

6 or 7 medium red
  potatoes
5 tablespoons unsalted
  butter
⅓ cup scallions, sliced
3 tablespoons flour
1½ cups chicken broth
1 teaspoon caraway seeds
½ teaspoon crushed cumin
  seeds
Salt and white pepper,
  to taste
2 cups grated Swiss cheese
½ cup bread crumbs
½ teaspoon paprika

Some folks peel their potatoes; others like the added texture and flavor of the peel. Either way, here's a quick recipe for a potato hankering: Boil 10 white potatoes, cool, and grate. Layer potatoes twice in a nonmetal baking dish, alternating with a pound of grated Cheddar, ¼ cup grated Parmesan, a bunch of chopped scallions, and generous dots of unsalted butter. Drizzle a pint of cream over the top and bake 30 minutes uncovered at 350 degrees. Serves 6.

Preheat oven to 400 degrees. Boil unpeeled potatoes until tender. Drain and cool. Cut into half-inch cubes and place in a buttered casserole dish (8½ x 13 inches).

In a separate pan, melt three tablespoons butter and saute scallions until tender. Add flour and broth, stirring until thick and bubbly. Stir in caraway seeds, cumin, salt, and pepper. Pour sauce over potatoes and top with cheese. Melt remaining butter and brown the bread crumbs. Stir in paprika and sprinkle mixture over the cheese. (Casserole may be covered and refrigerated at this point.)

Bake 20 minutes (35 minutes if chilled) or until lightly browned on top. Allow to cool slightly before serving.

YIELD: 4 TO 6 SERVINGS

BARBECUED CONFETTI VEGETABLES

A colorful and tasty sideline for barbecued meats.
This recipe can easily be doubled.

1½ cups yellow corn,
  cut fresh from cobs
8 to 10 firm cherry
  tomatoes, halved
½ medium green pepper,
  julienned
1 sweet red pepper,
  julienned
1 small onion, sliced
1 tablespoon chopped fresh
  basil
Salt and freshly ground
  pepper, to taste
¼ teaspoon grated lemon
  rind
4 teaspoons unsalted butter

Mix all ingredients, except butter, in a large bowl. Place half the mixture (or enough for two servings) in a foot-square piece of foil. Top with two teaspoons butter. Bring up corners of foil over vegetables and crumple ends together to form a pyramid. Close any gaps but allow room for hot air to circulate during grilling. Repeat for remaining vegetables.

Grill over medium-hot coals 20 to 30 minutes or until vegetables are tender.

YIELD: 4 SERVINGS

Onions and robust meats— it's a marriage of flavors that has become traditional. For a quick dish of sauteed onions, slice 4 onions very thin and saute in butter with a dash or two of paprika and salt. When onions are tender, stir in 2 teaspoons brown sugar, cover pan, and cook 15 minutes or until lightly browned. Serves 4.

RISOTTO

This recipe varies easily to complement different entrees. Add a tablespoon or two of a chopped fresh herb in place of saffron, for example. Or for extra texture, toast a handful of pine nuts and add once the rice has cooked.

¼ cup olive oil
6 tablespoons unsalted
  butter
1 large onion, finely
  chopped
1 clove garlic, minced
2 cups rice (Italian Riso
  Arborio preferred)
Saffron threads
7 cups broth
½ cup dry white wine
1 cup freshly grated
  Parmesan cheese

Heat oil and four tablespoons of the butter in a large saucepan (four-quart capacity) over medium heat. Saute onion until transparent. Add garlic and rice and stir three minutes or so, until rice turns milky and opaque. Stir in saffron, about one-eighth teaspoon, or more to taste. Add broth and wine and cook uncovered, stirring occasionally, until mixture comes to a boil. Reduce heat until rice boils gently. Cook until rice is just tender and most of the liquid has been absorbed, about 20 to 25 minutes. Stir occasionally during the last few minutes of cooking time to prevent sticking. Remove from heat, stir in cheese and remaining butter.

YIELD: 6 SERVINGS

*Brides and groc
showered with :
Western traditic
ancient associat
rice with fertilit
about 2500 var
feeds half the w
basic kinds are ,
which is short-g
sticky and moist
and Indian rice,
less starch and i
flakier when coo
verted rice is the
milling process, i
2000 years, whic
greater retention
than for regular*

Saffron, the world's most expensive spice, was used in ancient times as a perfume, dye, and medicine. Saffron threads are the stigma, or pollen-collecting part, of a Mediterranean crocus. It is harvested by hand, and a single flower contributes three stigmas. It takes thirteen thousand stigmas to yield one ounce of the spice.

RI(

A d(
For :
cook

½ cu
1 cu|
  int(
2 cu|
2 cu|
1 cu|
1 cu|
  toa:
Salt a
  pep

In a s
vermi(

Heat l
Add r
simme
absorb
and p(

YIELD

LEMON RICE

With long-grain rice, this dish is very light and goes well with seafood. For a nuttier, richer flavor, suitable for red meats or spicy chicken, substitute wild rice, increase the water by one cup and the cooking time by ten minutes.

1 cup long-grain rice
2½ cups water
½ teaspoon salt
1 teaspoon grated lemon
  peel
1 tablespoon fresh lemon
  juice
1 tablespoon unsalted
  butter
2 tablespoons minced
  flat-leaf parsley

In a 1½-quart saucepan with a tightly fitting lid, combine rice with water and salt and bring to a boil. Cover and simmer 20 to 30 minutes, until moisture is absorbed. Stir in lemon peel, juice, butter, and parsley. Cover and let stand five minutes. Fluff and serve.

YIELD: 6 SERVINGS

Now, along with Minnesota, California can boast its own successful wild rice crop. This grain's distinctive nutty flavor requires little for enhancement. Lightly buttered, and with fresh herbs, wild rice provides a savory nest for meat entrees. Combined with sauteed onion and celery, it can spruce up scrambled eggs. And for a richly flavored combination, add chopped walnuts, sherry, sage, and a bit of cream.

HOMEMADE PASTA

The amount of flour needed will vary with the size of the eggs and the day's humidity. Start with the measurement given, and adjust as needed. Toss pasta in one of the sauces on page 178.

1½ cups flour
¼ teaspoon salt
2 large eggs

One of the wonders of pasta is how deliciously it accepts cheese. A rich pasta treat for cheese lovers includes these four cheeses: Gorgonzola, Bel Paese, Fontina (or Swiss), and Parmesan. Cook a pound of pasta al dente and toss in a half cup of melted unsalted butter. Mix with a little less than a half cup of each of the cheeses listed (crumbled, grated, shredded), toss gently, and sprinkle with freshly ground black pepper. Serves 4 to 6.

Mix flour and salt together and shape into a mound on a hard surface. Make a well in the center, break eggs into the well, and beat eggs slightly with a fork. Mix flour into eggs with a circular motion, taking flour from the inside wall of the well. Support the outside of the mound with your free hand as you mix, to keep the wall from collapsing.

When eggs are no longer runny, sprinkle the flour over them and begin working the dough with palms and fingertips. Push and squeeze in a kneading motion. Add enough flour to form a firm, elastic ball.

Roll out dough and cut into fettuccine width, a little less than ¼ inch. Allow to dry on clean towels. Heat a large pot of water to a rapid boil. Let pasta slide off towels into water. Cook one to two minutes until just tender. Drain.

YIELD: 4 SERVINGS

LINGURIAN LASAGNE WITH PESTO

If you make your own pasta for this recipe, puree a red pepper and add to dough.

1 pound lasagne noodles
   (red pepper, preferred)
2 bunches fresh basil
2 cloves garlic
⅓ cup pine nuts
5 tablespoons freshly grated
   Parmesan cheese
3 tablespoons freshly grated
   Romano cheese
½ cup olive oil
2 sprigs parsley
Salt and freshly ground
   pepper, to taste

6 tablespoons butter
6 tablespoons flour
3 cups milk, heated
Salt and freshly ground
   pepper, to taste
2 tablespoons chopped
   fresh parsley
½ onion, finely chopped
2 tablespoons olive oil
4 ounces sun-dried
   tomatoes

Preheat oven to 400 degrees. Cook noodles until just tender. Douse in cold water and set aside to drain.

To prepare pesto, put basil, garlic, pine nuts, and cheese in a food processor and blend to a paste. Add olive oil and parsley. Blend. Season to taste with salt and pepper. Set aside.

In a saucepan, melt butter and stir in flour. Stir constantly over low heat until mixture bubbles gently one minute. Add milk all at once and whisk until sauce is smooth. Season with salt and pepper. Remove from heat and add parsley. In a separate saucepan, saute onion in olive oil until tender. Add sun-dried tomatoes, cover, and cook five minutes. Add this mixture to white sauce and fold in gently.

Place a layer of noodles in the bottom of a baking dish (8 x 12 inches). Top with pesto and white sauce. Repeat. Finish with a layer of noodles topped with white sauce. Bake 15 to 20 minutes or just enough to heat thoroughly. Allow to stand at least 10 minutes before serving.

YIELD: 6 SERVINGS

Tomatoes dried in the sun have a concentrated flavor. Sun-dried tomatoes are prepared in a technique similar to the way grapes are turned to raisins, and just as raisins don't taste exactly like grapes, sun-dried tomatoes also differ in flavor from tomatoes. Look for a very red color, not brown, and select a variety packed in oil, which is essential for the best flavor and tenderness.

SPINACH LASAGNE

2 tablespoons olive oil
1 onion, chopped
1 clove garlic, finely
  chopped
4 cups tomato sauce
1 tablespoon mixed dried
  herbs (marjoram, thyme,
  rosemary, savory, sage,
  oregano, and basil,
  for example)
1 pound ricotta cheese

1 pound mozzarella cheese,
  shredded
1 egg
1¼ cups fresh spinach,
  cooked
1 teaspoon salt
¾ teaspoon dried oregano
Freshly ground pepper,
  to taste
½ pound lasagne noodles
1 cup water

Heat olive oil and saute onion and garlic until tender. Add tomato sauce, cover and simmer 20 minutes. Add herb mixture, reduce heat, and cook an additional 10 minutes. Pour a half cup of the sauce to cover the bottom of a buttered baking dish (13 x 9 inches).

Preheat oven to 350 degrees. In a large bowl, mix ricotta, all but a fourth of the mozzarella, egg, spinach, salt, oregano, and pepper. Put a layer of uncooked noodles on top of the sauce in the baking dish and top with half of the cheese mixture. Repeat layers. Top with remaining noodles, sauce, and sprinkle with reserve mozzarella. Pour water around edges of dish, cover tightly with foil, and bake one hour and 15 minutes or until bubbly. Allow to cool at least 15 minutes before serving.

YIELD: 6 SERVINGS

PASTA WITH BROCCOLI SAUCE

1 bunch broccoli
2 cloves garlic
½ cup chopped fresh basil
2 tablespoons pine nuts
4 tablespoons freshly grated
  Parmesan cheese
½ cup olive oil
1 pound spaghettini
2 ripe tomatoes, peeled,
  seeded, and chopped
Chopped fresh basil
  (garnish)

Cut florets and small stems from broccoli. Cook in a pot
of boiling salted water until tender. Drain and douse in
cold water. Place in a food processor with garlic, basil, pine
nuts, and cheese. Puree and add olive oil slowly as
machine runs.

Cook spaghettini in a large pot of rapidly boiling water.
Drain and toss with broccoli sauce. Serve on warmed
plates with tomatoes on top. Sprinkle with basil.

YIELD: 6 SERVINGS

FETTUCCINE WITH SMOKED SALMON SAUCE

¼ cup unsalted butter
½ pound smoked salmon,
  coarsely chopped
1 teaspoon snipped fresh
  dill
1 cup heavy cream
1 pound fettuccine
1½ cups broccoli, steamed
  and chopped
½ cup freshly grated
  Parmesan cheese
Freshly ground pepper,
  to taste

Melt butter and saute salmon for one minute. Add dill and cream and cook over medium heat, stirring constantly, until cream is slightly reduced, about 10 minutes. Do not boil. Remove from heat and keep warm.

Cook pasta in rapidly boiling salted water. Drain and transfer to a warm bowl. Add broccoli, cheese, cream sauce, and pepper. Toss gently and serve immediately.

YIELD: 4 TO 6 SERVINGS

VEGETABLE FETTUCCINE CARBONARA

4 eggs
¼ cup heavy cream
8 strips bacon
½ cup sliced fresh
  mushrooms
½ cup sliced carrots
½ cup chopped cauliflower
½ cup peas
½ cup sliced zucchini
½ cup sliced green pepper

¼ cup chopped scallions
1 clove garlic, finely
  chopped
1 pound fettuccine
¼ cup unsalted butter,
  cut into pats
1 cup freshly grated
  Parmesan cheese
Salt and freshly ground
  pepper, to taste

Beat eggs with cream in a small bowl and set aside. Cook bacon in a heavy skillet until crisp. Remove bacon, drain, and set aside. Saute mushrooms, carrots, cauliflower, peas, zucchini, peppers, scallions, and garlic in bacon drippings five or more minutes or until crisp-tender. Remove from pan to drain.

Cook fettuccine in rapidly boiling water until tender. Drain and transfer to a large bowl. Add butter and toss to coat. Stir in egg mixture. Add vegetables, crumble the bacon and add with cheese, tossing gently. Season with salt and pepper and serve immediately.

YIELD: 6 TO 8 SERVINGS

From an anatomical stand-point, eggplant, peppers, pea pods, beans, cucumbers, and the kernels of corn are actually fruit. A banana is a berry. Broccoli, like cauliflower, is a mass of flowers (hence florets), and the unbloomed flowers of an artichoke are the tough bed of strings inside—the choke.

SPAGHETTINI PRIMAVERA

4 tablespoons olive oil
1 pound mild Italian
  sausage
2 dried hot chili peppers
3½ cups plum tomatoes,
  cooked, peeled, and
  chopped
¾ cup minced flat-leaf
  parsley
2 cloves garlic, minced

3 sweet red peppers,
  roasted, peeled, and
  sliced
1 sprig fresh oregano
Salt and freshly ground
  pepper, to taste
¾ pound spaghettini
¼ cup freshly grated
  Parmesan cheese
¼ cup chopped fresh basil

Fresh, ripe tomatoes, with taste, are always preferred but they are summer fare. Off-season tomatoes are rarely flavorful. Substitute canned Italian plum tomatoes in cooked dishes. One pound of ripe tomatoes equals 2 cups canned, cooked for ten minutes to reduce the liquid and enhance the taste.

Heat half the oil in a large, heavy skillet over medium heat. Add sausage and cook partially covered until brown, about 20 minutes. Remove from pan and set aside.

Discard all but one tablespoon of fat. Add remaining olive oil and increase heat to medium-high. Saute chili peppers until skins turn black. Discard peppers and add tomatoes, parsley, and garlic to skillet. Bring to simmer, reduce heat, and add sweet peppers, oregano, salt and pepper. Cover and simmer gently 15 minutes, stirring occasionally to prevent burning. Cut sausages into thin slices and add to skillet. Reduce heat and keep skillet partially covered.

Bring a large kettle of salted water to a boil. Add spaghettini and cook until just tender. Drain and douse immediately with cold water. Add to skillet and toss. Serve on warmed plates and garnish with Parmesan cheese and basil.

YIELD: 4 TO 6 SERVINGS

LINGUINE WITH SPRING VEGETABLES

2 tablespoons olive oil
½ cup unsalted butter
1 medium onion, minced
2 cloves garlic, minced
½ pound mushrooms,
  thinly sliced
2 small zucchini,
  thinly sliced
1 carrot, julienned
1 pound early asparagus,
  sliced on diagonal
½ cup chicken broth

1 cup heavy cream
2 to 3 teaspoons dried basil
1 cup broccoli florets
3 scallions, thinly sliced
Salt and freshly ground
  pepper, to taste
1 pound linguine, cooked,
  drained, and warm
½ cup freshly grated
  Parmesan cheese
¼ cup minced fresh
  flat-leaf parsley

Preheat wok to medium-high heat. Add oil and butter and stir-fry onions and garlic until tender. Add mushrooms, zucchini, carrot, and asparagus, and stir-fry two to three minutes. Add chicken broth and cream. Cook several minutes until liquid is reduced, but do not boil. Add basil, broccoli, and scallions. Season with salt and pepper and cook one minute more. Add pasta and cheese. Mix gently but thoroughly. Serve on heated plates and sprinkle with minced parsley.

YIELD: 4 TO 6 SERVINGS

ANGEL HAIR PASTA WITH SHRIMP AND FETA CHEESE

1 pound shrimp, cooked,
   shelled, and deveined
1 pound feta cheese,
   rinsed, dried, and
   crumbled
6 scallions, finely chopped
4 teaspoons fresh oregano
4 tomatoes, peeled, seeded,
   and coarsely diced
Salt and freshly ground
   pepper, to taste
1 pound angel hair pasta,
   cooked and drained

Tomatoes can be peeled easily and quickly. For those with gas stoves, pierce a tomato with a long-handled fork and rotate the tomato over the flame until the skin darkens and blisters. It's then ready to peel. Otherwise, heat a pot of water to a rolling boil, add tomatoes, and remove pot from heat. Let stand one minute. Plunge tomatoes in very cold water, then peel.

Combine all ingredients except pasta. Let stand at room temperature one hour or more.

Add pasta to mixture and toss. (Can be refrigerated at this point, then brought to room temperature before serving.)

YIELD: 4 SERVINGS

FILLET OF SEA BASS WITH FRESH BASIL BUTTER

Don and Arlene Coulon, owner's of San Diego's long-established Belgian Lion, provide this selection from their menu. It is truly elegant in its simplicity.

**6 sea bass fillets, about
  6 ounces each
Flour, to coat
½ cup unsalted butter
Salt and freshly ground
  pepper, to taste
Juice of 1 lemon
Bunch basil, rinsed and
  coarsely chopped**

Preheat oven to 400 degrees. Coat fillets in flour and shake off excess. Melt two tablespoons of butter in a heavy cast iron skillet over medium heat. Salt and pepper three fillets and saute three minutes on each side. Repeat with additional butter and remaining fish. Place fish in a baking pan and finish cooking in oven. Depending on the thickness of the fillets, cooking time will take between 10 and 15 minutes. Do not overcook. The fish should stay moist without browning. Remove fish from pan and keep warm on a platter. Reserve cooking juices.

In a saucepan, melt remaining butter, add lemon juice and cooking juices. Whisk well. Add a little salt and basil. Heat just enough to wilt basil but not to cook it. Do not brown. Pour basil butter on sea bass and serve.

YIELD: 6 SERVINGS

Herb butters are great finishes for grilled or broiled fish, adding a touch of fresh flavor. Use a food processor and combine ½ cup unsalted butter with several leaves fresh tarragon—about one tablespoon chopped—or with basil, marjoram, or Italian parsley. For dill butter, combine three tablespoons snipped fresh dill with a squeeze of lemon juice and a dab of mustard, blended with ½ cup butter. Add a few capers or peppercorns, if you like, and taste as you create.

RED SNAPPER IN SEAFOOD SHERRY SAUCE

3 pounds snapper fillets
1 tablespoon paprika
Salt and freshly ground
    black pepper, to taste
2 tablespoons butter
½ cup butter, melted
3 cloves garlic, minced
3 scallions, chopped
2 tablespoons chopped
    fresh parsley

1 dozen or more large
    mushrooms, sliced
1 tablespoon flour
2 tablespoons freshly grated
    Parmesan cheese
½ cup sherry
1 pound small shrimp,
    cooked, shelled, and
    deveined
½ pound fresh white
    crabmeat

Fish markets store fresh fish on ice, which is the best way to preserve freshness. Rinse your fresh fish under cold water, pat dry, place it in a tightly sealed plastic bag, and immerse it in a bowl of ice water in the refrigerator. Use fish on the day you buy it, if at all possible.

Preheat oven to 350 degrees. Season fillets with paprika, salt, and pepper. Dot with two tablespoons butter, broken into pieces, and bake in a large, shallow pan 10 to 15 minutes until barely done. Remove from oven.

In melted butter, saute garlic and scallions over medium heat until tender. Add parsley and mushrooms. Brown slightly. Stir in flour, add cheese and sherry, stir briskly, and let simmer until sauce thickens slightly. Add shrimp and crabmeat, mixing well. Pour over baked fish and broil until lightly browned, about five minutes.

YIELD: 6 TO 8 SERVINGS

RED SNAPPER WITH LEMON CAPER BUTTER

2 pounds snapper fillets
2 teaspoons capers
¼ cup unsalted butter
Lemon juice, to taste

When the caper jar is empty, we use green peppercorns instead. The proportion and preparation stays the same, but the flavor is more intense.

Rinse fillets and pat dry. Place on a foil-lined broiler pan. Mash or chop capers, adding caper juice from bottle, if desired. Melt butter, add capers and lemon juice. Whisk together and spoon over fish. Broil or grill, turning once and basting, until golden.

YIELD: 4 SERVINGS

BAKED SHRIMP IN DILL SAUCE

6 large mushrooms,
   julienned
1 tablespoon finely
   chopped onion
¼ cup unsalted butter
1 tablespoon flour
1 tablespoon snipped fresh
   dill
½ cup chicken broth
½ cup cream

Juice of ½ lemon
Salt and freshly ground
   pepper, to taste
2 tablespoons dry white
   wine
1 pound shrimp, cooked,
   shelled, and deveined
2 cups cooked rice
Dill sprigs (garnish)

Preheat oven to 325 degrees. Saute mushrooms and
onions in melted butter over medium heat. Stir in flour
and dill, mixing well. Add broth and cream, bring to a
boil, add lemon juice, salt, pepper, and wine. Reduce heat
and simmer until sauce thickens slightly. Add shrimp.

Put rice in the bottom of a buttered baking dish and pour
shrimp and sauce on top. Bake 15 minutes. Do not overcook. Serve warm with sprigs of dill for garnish.

YIELD: 4 SERVINGS

ORANGE ROUGHY WITH BANANAS

4 large orange roughy
   fillets
Flour, to coat
Salt, freshly ground pepper,
   and paprika, to taste
¼ cup unsalted butter
½ cup dry sherry
2 tablespoons freshly
   squeezed lemon juice

2 tablespoons brown sugar
½ teaspoon ground ginger
2 bananas, quartered
   lengthwise
½ cup toasted slivered
   almonds

Dredge fillets in flour, shake off excess, and season with
salt, pepper, and paprika. Melt butter in a large skillet.
Saute fillets, about five minutes each side, or until flaky
and golden. Remove fillets and keep warm.

Drain skillet of all but about two tablespoons butter. Add
sherry, lemon juice, sugar, ginger, and bananas. Simmer
two minutes. Place fish on warm serving plates. Arrange
bananas around fish. Top with sauce and almonds.

YIELD: 4 SERVINGS

SPICY SHRIMP IN TOMATO HERB SAUCE

A dish with a touch of fire. Serve over rice or vermicelli. For variation, substitute one pound calamari (squid), sliced into bitesize pieces.

⅓ cup unsalted butter
4 cloves garlic, minced
2 dried red peppers
1 pound fresh shrimp,
  shelled and deveined
¼ cup flour
1 cup hot water
2 ripe tomatoes, peeled
  and chopped
8 ounces tomato sauce
½ cup scallion tops,
  chopped
½ cup chopped fresh
  parsley
¼ cup diced green pepper

1 teaspoon salt
2 bay leaves
½ teaspoon crushed thyme
2 tablespoons chopped
  fresh basil
1 lemon wedge
Cayenne pepper, to taste

All shrimp headed for the market is deheaded and frozen for shipping. Shrimp can be pink or gray depending on where they were caught. Color does not indicate freshness. To check shrimp for the best condition, snap one in half in its shell. The break should be crisp and the inside smell should be clean and sweet, not fishy.

Melt butter in a large skillet over medium heat and saute garlic and peppers one to two minutes. Add shrimp and saute until just opaque. Remove shrimp and set aside. Discard peppers.

Stir flour into skillet and cook until brown, stirring constantly for five minutes or more. Add water and tomatoes and cook until sauce thickens. Pour in tomato sauce, stir, add remaining ingredients, cover and simmer over low heat 15 minutes. Add shrimp back to skillet and simmer, uncovered, an additional five minutes. Remove bay leaves and lemon wedge before serving.

YIELD: 4 SERVINGS

BAY SCALLOPS BAKED IN GARLIC BUTTER

For a delicious taste and superb presentation, serve over freshly cooked angel hair pasta.

1 cup unsalted butter
1 cup bread crumbs
6 garlic cloves, crushed
¼ cup minced scallions
½ cup chopped flat-leaf
  parsley
¼ cup dry white wine
Juice of ½ lemon
Salt and freshly ground
  pepper, to taste
2 tablespoons olive oil
1½ pounds fresh bay
  scallops

Blend together butter, bread crumbs, garlic, two tablespoons minced scallions, parsley, wine, and lemon juice. Add a dash or two of salt and pepper. Form into a roll and wrap in waxed paper. Chill until firm, about one hour.

Preheat oven to 450 degrees. Heat oil in a large skillet over medium heat. Add remaining scallions and saute. Do not brown. Add scallops and salt and pepper to taste. Saute about five minutes. Drain liquid and arrange scallops in a shallow, buttered baking dish. Slice garlic butter and place slices evenly spaced over scallops. Bake until butter is hot and bubbly, about five to seven minutes. Serve immediately.

YIELD: 4 SERVINGS

ZARZUELA

This is one of those versatile dishes in which variations are easy and experiments are forgiving. Any firm fish can be used—fresh albacore, sea bass, or yellowtail, for example.

1 pound clams,
   well scrubbed
1 pound raw shrimp
1 pound fresh fish fillets,
   cut into large pieces
¼ pound scallops
3 tablespoons olive oil
1½ cups finely chopped
   onion
2 cloves garlic, minced
1 cup rice, uncooked
½ cup chopped fresh
   parsley

16 ounces Italian plum
   tomatoes, coarsely
   chopped, with liquid
12 ounces clam juice
½ cup dry red wine
1 cup water
2 tablespoons chopped
   cilantro
Dash Tabasco
Salt and freshly ground
   pepper, to taste
Avocado slices, sour cream,
   and cilantro (garnish)
Lime wedges

Clam season in California ranges from November through April, when many varieties are available—from the large geoducks to small butter clams. No matter how they are served, clams should be thoroughly cleaned before any preparation. Scrub the shells well under cold water and place them in a pot of cold salted water. Let stand several hours, rinse with cold fresh water, and discard any clams that open.

Steam seafood separately until just cooked. Remove clams from shells (discarding any that do not open), peel and devein shrimp. Set seafood aside.

Heat oil in a saucepan over medium heat and saute onion and garlic until tender. Stir in rice and parsley and cook until rice is golden brown. Add tomatoes, clam juice, wine, and water. Bring to a boil, cover, reduce heat and simmer 15 minutes.

Mix seafood into rice, add cilantro and Tabasco, cover and cook on low heat an additional 10 minutes. Check seasoning and salt and pepper to taste. Pour into shallow serving dish, top with avocado slices, dollops of sour cream, and sprigs of cilantro. Serve with lime wedges.

YIELD: 6 SERVINGS

CRAB STUFFED CHICKEN BREASTS IN THYME SAUCE

**4 boneless chicken breasts,
split and skinned**

Stuffing:

**10 ounces fresh crabmeat,
cooked and flaked**
**⅓ cup chopped flat-leaf
parsley**
⅓ cup soft bread crumbs
**1 cup shredded Swiss
cheese**

Sauce:

¼ cup unsalted butter
**¾ cup scallions and tops,
thinly sliced**
**½ pound mushrooms,
thinly sliced**
¼ cup flour
**2 tablespoons chopped
fresh thyme**
½ cup chicken broth
½ cup milk
1 cup dry white wine
**Salt and freshly ground
pepper, to taste**
**Flat-leaf parsley sprigs
(garnish)**

Preheat oven to 400 degrees. Pound chicken breasts until very thin. Set aside.

Combine stuffing ingredients in a bowl, reserving ¼ cup cheese. Mix well and set aside. To prepare sauce, melt butter in a saucepan over medium heat and saute scallions and mushrooms until tender. Stir in flour and thyme. Add broth and milk, stirring constantly. Add wine, salt, and pepper and stir until sauce is thoroughly heated. Remove from heat and add ¼ cup to stuffing mixture, mixing well.

Season chicken lightly with salt and pepper. Spoon stuffing mixture in the center of each breast, roll up, and place seam side down in a buttered baking dish. (Breasts may be covered and refrigerated at this point for advance preparation.)

Bake 30 to 40 minutes or until meat is no longer pink. Remove from oven, sprinkle with reserve cheese, and bake an additional five minutes. Whisk sauce and pour onto warmed serving plates, top with chicken, and garnish with sprigs of parsley.

YIELD: 6 TO 8 SERVINGS

Thyme, through time, has had many uses outside of cooking—as a fumigant, antiseptic, or mouthwash, for example. In the Middle Ages, sleeping on a pillow stuffed with thyme was thought to relieve melancholy. We're tempted to try it.

CHICKEN BREASTS WRAPPED IN RED CABBAGE

From Scott Meskan, Chef at George's at the Cove, La Jolla, comes this attractive entree. He suggests a quality 1982 Chardonnay as an ideal accompaniment.

4 chicken breasts, boneless and skinless
2 tablespoons unsalted butter
3 large carrots, julienned
1 bunch cilantro, chopped
¼ cup white wine
1½ cups rich chicken stock
1 large red cabbage, outside leaves only
Cooked rice

Pound chicken breasts flat. Cut each into a square shape and set aside. Melt butter in a saute pan and saute carrots, cilantro, and any chicken scraps about four minutes. Mix together white wine and ½ cup of chicken stock and add to pan. Cook until liquid is almost gone. Remove from heat and allow to cool.

Lay chicken breasts flat and spoon carrot mixture on edge of each breast. Roll up. Take one cabbage leaf, place a rolled breast on the edge and roll again. Tie with string at each end and trim off ends of cabbage. Poach the rolls in remaining cup of chicken stock.

To serve, cut string and discard. Cut each roll into five slices and place on a bed of hot rice.

YIELD: 4 SERVINGS

CHICKEN BREASTS WITH SPINACH CHEESE STUFFING

¾ pound fresh spinach
1 cup ricotta cheese
2 eggs, lightly beaten
½ cup freshly grated
  Parmesan cheese
1 teaspoon salt
Pepper, to taste

2 cloves garlic, minced
Dash of dried oregano,
  thyme, and rosemary
6 boneless chicken breasts,
  split, skins on
Olive oil

Preheat oven to 350 degrees. Steam spinach until soft, about five minutes. Cool and squeeze out liquid. Chop finely or puree in a blender or food processor. Combine spinach in a bowl with ricotta, eggs, Parmesan, salt, pepper, garlic, and herbs. Mix well and stuff chicken breasts, in even portions, under skins. Brush skins with olive oil and sprinkle with additional oregano, thyme, and rosemary. Bake 15 minutes covered. Uncover and bake 25 minutes or until meat is no longer pink.
YIELD: 8 TO 10 SERVINGS

CHICKEN AND PROSCIUTTO

4 boneless chicken breasts
Salt, freshly ground pepper,
  and dried oregano
Flour, to coat
3 tablespoons unsalted
  butter
2 tablespoons olive oil
8 thin slices prosciutto

8 slices Bel Paese cheese
  or baby Swiss cheese
2 tablespoons freshly grated
  Parmesan cheese
2 tablespoons chicken
  broth
Sun-dried tomatoes and
  flat-leaf parsley (garnish)

Preheat oven to 350 degrees. Bring breasts to room temperature, remove skins, and cut in half. Pound until very thin. Rub salt, pepper, and oregano into meat. Dredge in flour and shake off excess. Heat butter and oil in a heavy skillet over moderate heat until very hot. Saute chicken to a light golden color but do not cook completely. Remove from skillet and place in a shallow baking dish.

Place a slice of prosciutto and cheese on each breast. Sprinkle with Parmesan. Pour oil off skillet but do not wipe. Add broth and heat, stirring just long enough to remove brown particles from pan. Pour broth over chicken, bake uncovered 20 minutes, or until cheese melts and is slightly browned. Place breasts on serving plates. Garnish with sun-dried tomatoes and sprigs of parsley.

YIELD: 4 SERVINGS

Ham cured in brine, then aged and dried, is the wonderful prosciutto. This meat should not be greasy, and the nutty flavor should have hints of salt and pepper. Look for prosciutto with a reddish color and a light gloss.

CHICKEN CURRY WITH TART APPLES AND AVOCADO

¼ cup unsalted butter
1 tablespoon curry powder
¾ cup chopped tart apples
¼ cup finely chopped
  onion
1 clove garlic, minced
Salt, to taste
¼ cup flour

½ cup plain yogurt
½ cup cream
1 cup chicken stock
2 cups cooked chicken,
  shredded
3 cups cooked rice
4 avocados, peeled and
  sliced

Preheat oven to 350 degrees. Melt butter in a large saucepan over medium heat. Stir in curry powder and saute apples, onions, and garlic until tender. Salt to taste. Stir in flour, add yogurt, cream, and stock gradually, mixing well after each. Cook until sauce is smooth and thick, stirring constantly. Add chicken.

Place cooked rice in the bottom of a shallow, buttered baking dish. Top with avocado slices followed by chicken mixture. Bake 10 minutes, uncovered.

YIELD: 6 TO 8 SERVINGS

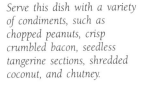

Serve this dish with a variety of condiments, such as chopped peanuts, crisp crumbled bacon, seedless tangerine sections, shredded coconut, and chutney.

CHINESE CHICKEN WITH ASPARAGUS

½ cup chicken stock
¼ cup Chinese cooking
  wine (Shao Hsing) or
  dry sherry
¼ cup soy sauce
1 teaspoon chopped garlic
1 teaspoon chopped ginger
  root
2 tablespoons cornstarch

1 egg white
5 boneless chicken breast
  halves, skinned, cut into
  bitesize pieces
¼ cup peanut oil
2 pounds asparagus, tough
  ends removed, cut into
  1½ inch lengths

In a bowl, combine stock, wine, soy sauce, garlic, ginger, and one tablespoon cornstarch. Set aside.

Lightly whisk together remaining cornstarch and egg white. Toss chicken in mixture to cover pieces. Heat two tablespoons oil in wok until oil barely begins to smoke. Drain chicken and toss fry pieces until just done. Set aside. Heat remaining oil, add asparagus, and toss fry 90 seconds. (This should heat the asparagus but not cook it.) Return chicken to wok with asparagus and add stock mixture. Toss to coat. Allow sauce to thicken, about 10 to 15 seconds. Turn onto a warmed platter and serve immediately.

Like all dishes prepared in a wok, this delicious combination is most successful if all ingredients are "ready to go" before the stir fry.

YIELD: 2 TO 3 SERVINGS

BREAST OF CHICKEN WITH GOAT CHEESE, HONEY, AND THYME

Neil Stuart, executive chef at San Diego's Pacifica Grill, provides this recipe—it's simple to prepare and has a definite California flair.

4 whole boneless chicken
  breasts
6 ounces California goat
  cheese
2 tablespoons peanut oil
2 tablespoons chopped
  fresh thyme
6 ounces malt vinegar
6 ounces orange honey
¼ cup butter

Preheat oven to 350 degrees. Open chicken breasts and place skin side down. Place goat cheese in the center of each breast, leaving a border around the edges. Fold breasts to enclose cheese. Heat oil in a large ovenproof saute pan. Brown chicken on both sides and complete cooking in oven, approximately 10 minutes. Remove chicken from pan, reserving juices. Add thyme, vinegar, honey, and butter to pan and cook, stirring constantly, over medium-low heat until butter has melted and is thoroughly incorporated. Pour over chicken and serve immediately.

YIELD: 4 SERVINGS

Goat cheese, chevre, can be found these days in about 75 varieties, packed in various shapes and sizes, and varying in texture and taste. As goat cheese matures, the nippy, sour taste increases to one that is earthy and forceful, and the creamy texture hardens to a brittleness. Young or old, it has a distinct taste worthy of experimentation. Laura Chenel of Sonoma Valley produces California's most notable goat cheese, found in pyramids or round shapes, covered with herbs or pepper, or packed just plain.

ALMOND CHICKEN STIR FRY

Serve with steamed rice or with noodles—and chopsticks, of course.

1 cup whole almonds
3 tablespoons peanut oil
½ cup chopped scallions
  and tops
4 boneless chicken breasts,
  skinned and sliced
8 ounces bamboo shoots,
  drained
6 ounces water chestnuts,
  drained
1 English cucumber, thinly
  sliced
½ cup chicken stock
2 teaspoons dry sherry or
  Chinese cooking wine
1 teaspoon grated ginger
  root
1 teaspoon soy sauce
½ teaspoon cornstarch
Dash salt
Dash red pepper

Heat any saute pan or skillet first before adding oil or butter. Doing so prevents overheating the oil or burning it. This is especially applicable to stir fry cooking. Heat the wok until very hot, then add peanut oil, which tolerates higher heat than most oils. The technique also prevents food from sticking to the pan. The best woks, by the way, are made of iron or carbon steel, which are superior for holding and distributing heat.

Preheat oven to 400 degrees. Place almonds in a shallow pan and brown in oven, stirring often, 12 to 15 minutes. Chop half the almonds. Set aside.

Heat oil in wok until oil just begins to smoke. Add scallions and stir fry one minute. Add half the chicken; stir fry one minute. Add remaining chicken and repeat. Stir in bamboo shoots, water chestnuts, and chopped almonds, tossing mixture one minute. Repeat with cucumber. Add stock, sherry, ginger, and soy sauce. Stir in and heat one minute.

In a small bowl, mix cornstarch with a tablespoon of water. Stir mixture slowly into wok. Add salt and pepper, and stir until liquid thickens, about two minutes. Turn onto a warmed serving platter and top with whole almonds.

YIELD: 4 TO 6 SERVINGS

PEKING CHICKEN IN TORTILLAS

Slightly sweet and spicy, this delicious chicken is ideal for informal fare. Note that the chicken needs to marinate.

3 chickens, halved, 2½ pounds each	1 tablespoon rice vinegar
Salt and freshly ground	2 teaspoons soy sauce
pepper	Hoisin sauce
½ teaspoon cinnamon	1 bunch scallions and tops,
½ teaspoon ground ginger	chopped
1 tablespoon brown sugar	12 flour tortillas, cut in half and warmed

Bring several quarts of water to a boil in a large soup pot. Drop in chicken halves, one at a time, and boil one minute. Drain and pat dry. Season with salt and pepper.

Combine ¼ teaspoon pepper with cinnamon, ginger, sugar, vinegar, and soy sauce, mixing well. Brush chicken with mixture and refrigerate four to six hours.

Preheat oven to 350 degrees. Place chicken on cookie sheets and bake uncovered 50 to 60 minutes, or until no longer pink. Skin should be bubbly and browned. Allow to cool slightly before serving. Meat should be pulled off the bone, topped with Hoisin sauce and scallions, and wrapped in tortillas.

YIELD: 6 SERVINGS

BOK CHOY CHICKEN

6 tablespoons peanut oil	1½ pounds bok choy
½ pound boneless chicken	(Chinese greens), sliced
breast, skinned, cut into	on diagonal
bitesize pieces	½ cup chicken stock
4 teaspoons cornstarch	½ teaspoon salt
1 teaspoon sugar	

Heat three tablespoons peanut oil in a wok until oil barely begins to smoke. Toss chicken with two teaspoons cornstarch and sugar. Toss fry until just cooked. Remove from wok and set aside. Heat remaining oil, add bok choy and toss fry 30 seconds. Add chicken stock and salt and bring to a boil. Cover and steam one minute. Dissolve remaining cornstarch in one tablespoon of water. Return chicken to wok and mix with greens. Add cornstarch solution and toss to coat. Turn onto warm platter and serve immediately.

YIELD: 2 TO 3 SERVINGS

Bok choy's crunchy stalks have a mild flavor, juicy and almost sweet. The leafy portion tastes more like cabbage. Wrap heads, unwashed, in the refrigerator and plan to use this vegetable in just a few days. It is highly nutritious, low in calories, and a familiar stir fry ingredient.

MARINATED SESAME CHICKEN

Crispy, flavorful, and easy to prepare.

Marinade:

¼ cup soy sauce
1 tablespoon sugar
1 tablespoon dry sherry
1 tablespoon fresh ginger
   root, peeled and minced
2 cloves garlic, minced

12 chicken thighs
2 eggs, beaten
1 cup flour
¾ cup sesame seeds
2 tablespoons butter
2 tablespoons olive oil

Freshly grated or minced ginger has a distinct bite when raw. When cooked, the flavor sweetens and becomes more subdued, and the wonderful fragrance is released. Lively words such as zing, tang, punch, and spark amply describe its flavorful effects. Enticing applies to the affect on the atmosphere. Store fresh ginger in root form, unwrapped in the refrigerator. Wrapping it traps moisture, causing mold or deterioration.

Combine marinade ingredients, blending well. Pour marinade over chicken, covering all pieces, and let stand two hours. For advance preparation, marinate overnight in the refrigerator.

Preheat oven to 500 degrees. Place a shallow baking pan (10 x 15 inches) in oven.

Remove chicken from marinade. Add two tablespoons of marinade to eggs. On waxed paper, mix together flour and sesame seeds. Dip chicken in egg mixture and roll in flour mixture to coat.

Remove hot pan from oven and add butter and oil. Turn pan to melt butter and coat the bottom. Place thighs in pan and bake uncovered 15 minutes. Turn and cook an additional 15 minutes or until chicken is no longer pink.

YIELD: 6 SERVINGS

ROCK CORNISH HENS WITH LINGUINE AND VEGETABLES

2 Rock Cornish hens,
  1½ pounds each, split
2 medium leeks
4 small carrots
4 tablespoons olive oil
½ pound mushrooms,
  sliced
¼ teaspoon salt
1 pound spinach, rinsed,
  stems removed, and
  lightly steamed
1 chicken boullion cube
½ cup dry white wine
½ teaspoon dried thyme
½ pound linguine

Rinse hens and pat dry. Set aside.

Cut off roots of leeks and trim off leafy ends. Cut each leek in half lengthwise and separate into leaves. Rinse well. Julienne leeks and carrots. Heat two tablespoons oil in a skillet over medium heat. Saute leeks and carrots five minutes. Add mushrooms and salt and saute an additional three minutes, or until vegetables are tender. Toss in spinach and cook until heated through. Remove vegetables with a slotted spoon and set aside.

Heat skillet to medium high and add two tablespoons oil. Cook hens until browned on all sides, about 10 minutes. Stir in boullion, wine, and thyme and bring to a boil. Reduce heat to medium low, cover, and cook 20 minutes or until hens are fork tender. Season with salt, to taste.

Cook linguine in rapidly boiling water until just tender. Drain and place in saucepan. Remove hens from skillet and place on warmed serving plates. Pour liquid into saucepan with linguine. Add vegetables, stir, and cook briefly until heated through. Divide evenly between plates, top with hens, and serve immediately.

YIELD: 4 SERVINGS

The name Rock Cornish hen comes from the fact that the bird is a cross between two breeds: Plymouth Rock and Cornish. These hens are best fresh, not frozen. Scout around for a butcher who specializes in poultry, or check ethnic markets to find fresh ones. The difference in flavor is well worth the look.

HERB CHICKEN WITH GRAPES IN WINE SAUCE

3 tablespoons flour
2 teaspoons chopped fresh
  basil
2 teaspoons chopped fresh
  tarragon
¼ teaspoon paprika
Salt and freshly ground
  white pepper
2 boneless chicken breasts,
  split and skinned
1 tablespoon olive oil
1 tablespoon unsalted
  butter
2 cloves garlic, minced
½ cup dry white wine
1 cup red seedless grapes
½ cup chicken broth
1 teaspoon freshly squeezed
  lemon juice
Flat-leaf parsley sprigs
  (garnish)

Combine flour, basil, tarragon, paprika, salt, and pepper. Dredge breasts in mixture, coating all sides.

Heat oil and butter in a skillet over medium-high heat. Saute garlic briefly, add chicken and saute on both sides until golden brown. Reduce heat to low, pour in wine, and cook chicken five minutes or more, until no longer pink. Add grapes, broth, and lemon juice and cook until heated through, about five minutes. Remove chicken and grapes with a slotted spoon. Keep warm.

Increase heat and continue cooking sauce until reduced by half. Place chicken and grapes on warmed serving plates. Pour sauce over chicken and garnish with parsley.

YIELD: 4 SERVINGS

STUFFED CHICKEN BREASTS IN HERB BUTTER

3 boneless chicken breasts,
   split and skinned
½ cup unsalted butter,
   softened
Salt and freshly ground
   pepper
6 slices mozzarrella cheese
6 slices smoked ham
½ cup flour
1 egg, beaten
1 cup Italian bread crumbs
2 tablespoons chopped
   fresh parsley
1 teaspoon each of
   chopped fresh sage,
   rosemary, and thyme
½ cup dry white wine
Parsley sprigs (garnish)

Preheat oven to 325 degrees. Pound breasts to flatten. Spread one side of each breast with half of the butter and season with salt and pepper. Place one slice of cheese and ham on each, roll, and tuck ends. Secure with toothpicks. Dredge in flour to coat, shake off excess, dip in egg, and roll in bread crumbs. Place in a buttered shallow baking dish.

Melt remaining butter in a small saucepan over low heat. Stir in herbs, mixing well. Pour over chicken and bake 30 minutes, basting with herb butter. Pour wine over chicken, bake an additional 20 minutes, and baste with cooking juices. Serve on warmed plates and garnish with parsley.

YIELD: 6 SERVINGS

Chicken paillards, half breasts pounded until very thin, allow the meat to cook quickly and to readily absorb marinades and seasonings. The removal of skin and fat results in a healthful, light approach to chicken entrees. Here's one method for preparing paillards: Split a whole boned breast in half. Cut the membrane that attaches the smaller muscle to the breastbone, but leave the membrane on the rib side. Fold the smaller muscle back. Sprinkle the meat with a little oil, place between sheets of waxed paper or in a plastic bag, and pound with a mallet or the side of a heavy cleaver to flatten.

CHICKEN SAUTE WITH TART APPLES

¼ cup unsalted butter
2 tart apples, cored and
  thinly sliced
4 boneless chicken breasts,
  skinned and cut in half
Flour, to coat
1 large onion, finely
  chopped

⅓ cup dry sherry
⅓ cup apple juice
⅓ cup cream
Freshly ground pepper,
  to taste

Melt half the butter over medium heat in a skillet and saute apples until lightly browned. Remove from skillet.

Pound each breast to flatten. Dredge in flour and shake off excess. Melt remaining butter in skillet and saute chicken until browned, about 10 minutes. Remove from skillet and keep warm.

Add onions to skillet and saute until translucent. Return chicken to skillet, add sherry and apple juice. Cover and simmer over low heat 10 minutes. Remove chicken, pour cream into skillet and simmer uncovered, stirring constantly, about 10 minutes. Pour sauce onto serving plates, top with chicken and apples. Add pepper to taste.

YIELD: 4 SERVINGS

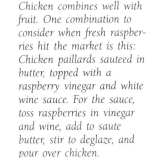

Chicken combines well with fruit. One combination to consider when fresh raspberries hit the market is this: Chicken paillards sauteed in butter, topped with a raspberry vinegar and white wine sauce. For the sauce, toss raspberries in vinegar and wine, add to saute butter, stir to deglaze, and pour over chicken.

JALAPENO STUFFED CHICKEN BREASTS

4 chicken breasts, split,
  skinned, and boned
2 ripe avocados, peeled,
  pitted, and quartered
14 ounces jalapeno
  peppers, drained
  (8 peppers)

8 slices Jack cheese,
  ¼ inch thick
2 eggs, beaten
1½ cups bread crumbs
2 tablespoons butter
2 tablespoons olive oil

Pound chicken breasts to flatten. Place one slice avocado, one jalapeno pepper, and one slice cheese on each breast. Roll and secure with toothpicks or poultry needles. Dip into eggs and coat with bread crumbs. Heat butter and oil in a skillet over medium-high heat. Saute until brown on all sides, reduce heat to low, cover, and simmer 20 minutes. Remove lid and cook an additional 5 to 10 minutes.

Chopped ripe tomatoes, avocado slices, and salsa are the ideal garnish for this Mexican-style chicken. Cilantro lovers can add fresh sprigs of cilantro for that extra, distinctively Mexican flavor.

YIELD: 4 SERVINGS

CHICKEN THIGHS BAKED WITH GINGER ROOT

Chicken Teriyaki is a popular Southern California entree. This recipe has similar overtones, is very easy to prepare, and will fill the kitchen with a magnificent aroma.

12 thick slices ginger root,
   unpeeled
12 chicken thighs, skins
   removed, room
   temperature
1 large onion, quartered
1 cup mayonnaise
1 cup soy sauce
Juice of ½ orange
¼ teaspoon cayenne pepper
Fresh pineapple slices and
   fresh mint sprigs
   (garnish)

Preheat oven to 350 degrees. Lightly butter a shallow baking pan. Place ginger root slices in pan, spaced out evenly. Place a chicken thigh on top of each slice. Break up onion wedges into pieces and sprinkle around chicken.

Whisk together (or shake in a jar) remaining ingredients. Pour over chicken, coating the tops of all thighs. Cover pan with foil and bake 15 minutes. Remove foil and bake an additional 15 minutes, or until chicken is tender and no longer pink. Place thighs, without ginger or onion, on warm serving plates. Garnish plates with pineapple and top each thigh with a sprig of mint.

YIELD: 6 SERVINGS

The mayonnaise in this recipe "bakes off," leaving no mayonnaise taste. It keeps the chicken moist and holds the soy sauce flavor as the meat cooks.

LEMON CHICKEN SCALLOPINI

Wild rice and steamed vegetables accompany this entree beautifully.

2 large chicken breasts,
  split, skinned, and boned
¾ teaspoon salt
½ teaspoon freshly ground
  pepper
4 teaspoons olive oil
4 teaspoons cornstarch
1 egg white
Flour, to coat

¼ cup unsalted butter
1 lemon, thinly sliced
2 tablespoons freshly
  squeezed lemon juice
1 clove garlic, minced
½ cup water
2 tablespoons chopped
  fresh parsley (garnish)

Pound each breast to flatten. Season with salt and pepper and place in a glass dish. Let stand 20 minutes. Rub oil into chicken with the back of a spoon and sprinkle with cornstarch. Let stand 20 minutes. Fold in egg white to cover all pieces. Let stand 30 minutes.

Shake off excess egg white. Coat chicken with flour and saute in butter over medium heat, until golden on outside and no longer pink in center, about five minutes each side. Remove from skillet and keep warm. Add lemon slices to pan and stir with drippings. Add lemon juice, garlic, and water to skillet. Cook over high heat, stirring constantly to thicken and reduce. Remove lemon slices and set aside. Pour sauce on warmed serving plates, top with chicken and lemon slices. Garnish with parsley.

YIELD: 4 SERVINGS

GRILLED CHICKEN WITH HERB MUSTARD

½ cup dry white wine
⅔ cup olive oil
6 tablespoons red wine
    vinegar
2 tablespoons chopped red
    onion
1 teaspoon salt
1 teaspoon each chopped
    fresh oregano, basil,
    chives
2 cloves garlic, minced
½ teaspoon freshly ground
    pepper
¼ cup spicy brown
    mustard
4 chicken breasts, split

Combine all ingredients, except chicken, and mix well.
Remove skin from chicken, if desired. Place chicken in a
shallow baking dish, pour in sauce, covering all pieces.
Cover and marinate four hours or overnight in the
refrigerator.

Grill chicken over medium coals, basting with sauce, about
40 minutes or until no longer pink.

YIELD: 6 TO 8 SERVINGS

*Barbecued chicken should
never be boring. Chicken is
probably the easiest meat to
grill, accepting the flavors of
most any marinade or
barbecue sauce. Grill breasts
bone side down for most of
the cooking time to help prevent moisture loss—bones
absorb heat more slowly
than meat.*

GRAPE SAUCE FOR ROAST POULTRY

You won't have to say "Enjoy" when you present a roast duck, pheasant, or range hen with this irresistible sauce. It goes without saying.

1¼ cups seedless grapes
6 tablespoons butter
1 cup quality port
¼ teaspoon ground cloves
1 teaspoon cornstarch
½ cup finely chopped
  pecans or roasted pine
  nuts

Combine grapes with a cup of water in a covered pan. Cook over medium heat three to five minutes. Drain and set aside.

Melt butter in a small saucepan. Stir in port and cloves. Add grapes. Cover and simmer five minutes. Dissolve cornstarch in ¼ cup water. Reduce heat to low, add cornstarch solution, and stir until sauce thickens. Add nuts. Pour sauce over slices of roast poultry.

YIELD: SAUCE FOR 6 SERVINGS

STUFFED BREAST OF VEAL

Stuffing:

2 sweetbreads
6 ounces ground pork
3 ounces chopped fat back
1 cup bread crumbs
½ cup milk
3 eggs, lightly beaten
4 shallots, minced
1 tablespoon butter
2 tablespoons chopped
    fresh parsley
1 teaspoon each salt,
    pepper, nutmeg

1 breast of veal (about
    5 pounds), boned
2 tablespoons olive oil
2 tablespoons butter
1 leek, washed, trimmed,
    chopped
2 carrots, sliced

1 rib celery, sliced
1 teaspoon thyme
2 cloves
1 bay leaf
6 cups chicken stock

Sauce:

3 tablespoons butter
1 tablespoon flour
1 cup cream
1 bunch spinach, washed
    and blanched, stems
    removed
1 tablespoon chopped fresh
    parsley
1 tablespoon chopped
    chives
1 teaspoon dried chervil
Juice of 1 lemon
Salt and freshly ground
    pepper, to taste

Blanch sweetbreads. Remove and discard membranes. Dice sweetbreads and combine with remaining stuffing ingredients. Mix well.

Cup a deep pocket into the breast, almost to the edge of the meat. Add stuffing, roll the breast, and use kitchen string to tie at one-inch intervals to close.

Preheat oven to 325 degrees. Heat oil and butter in a large skillet and brown the breast on both sides over medium-high heat. Remove breast and lightly saute leek, carrots, and celery. Place vegetables in the bottom of a large, buttered braising pan. Add breast, thyme, cloves, bay leaf, and stock. Cover pan and cook in the oven two hours (an inserted meat thermometer should read 170 degrees), or until done. Add more stock during cooking if liquid reduces too much.

Remove breast to a warm serving platter. Strain juices and reserve. To prepare sauce, melt butter in a saucepan and whisk in flour. Add pan juices and bring to a boil. Allow liquid to reduce. Reduce heat, add cream, spinach, and herbs. Puree, return to pan, add lemon juice and salt and pepper to taste. Slice breast and top with sauce to serve.

YIELD: 6 SERVINGS

Veal is regaining much of the popularity it held in the 1930s and 1940s. Milk-fed veal is considered the tenderest and most flavorful. Because the milk diet is very low in iron, this form of beef is a pale color, slightly pink, and lacks the red of more mature cuts.

VEAL CHOPS IN RED CHILI

Robert Brody, the Executive Chef at San Diego's Sheraton on Harbor Island, works wonders with veal. This is one of two delicious recipes he has given us for veal chops.

2 cloves garlic
8 tomatillos, peeled
4 10-ounce veal chops,
  trimmed of fat
⅓ cup flour, seasoned with
  salt, pepper, and paprika
¼ cup olive oil
3 cups chicken broth
3 tablespoons chili powder,
  pure ground, mild
½ cup tomato sauce
2 teaspoons sugar
¼ cup chopped fresh
  parsley
4 teaspoons sour cream
  (garnish)
2 tablespoons chopped
  scallions (garnish)

Puree garlic with tomatillos. Reserve. Dredge chops in the seasoned flour. Heat oil in a saute pan large enough to hold all four chops. Saute chops about five minutes on each side. Do not overcook or the meat will become tough and dry. Remove the chops and keep warm.

Add the garlic mixture, half the chicken stock, and the chili powder to the pan. Reduce by half. Add remaining stock, tomato sauce, and sugar. Bring to a boil, then reduce heat to simmer. Add parsley. Remove the pan from heat.

Place chops on serving dishes and spoon sauce on top. Garnish with sour cream and chopped scallions.

YIELD: 4 SERVINGS

SHERRIED VEAL

Boneless turkey breast can be substituted for veal with excellent result.

**1 pound veal scallops,
  pounded thin**
**Salt and freshly ground
  pepper**
Flour, to coat
⅓ cup unsalted butter
1 tablespoon olive oil
¾ cup dry sherry
Flat-leaf parsley (garnish)

Season veal with salt and pepper. Dredge in flour and shake off excess. Heat butter and oil in a skillet over medium-high heat. Saute veal two minutes each side or until done. Remove from skillet and keep warm.

Add sherry to skillet and boil one minute, stirring vigorously to deglaze. Remove from heat. Place veal on warm serving plates, top with sherry sauce, and garnish with sprigs of parsley.

YIELD: 4 SERVINGS

Deglazing is the addition of water, wine, or vinegar to a pan in which meat has been browned. A whisk is usually used to stir and scrape up the brown particles and to incorporate them into added butter or cream.

BAKED LAMB STEW WITH FRESH ROSEMARY

3½ pounds boneless lamb, cubed
3 tablespoons chopped fresh rosemary
½ teaspoon freshly ground pepper
2 cloves garlic, minced
1 onion, chopped
14 ounces chicken broth
¾ cup dry white wine

1½ pounds button mushrooms
1 pound pearl onions, peeled
12 small carrots
1 cup cream
1 tablespoon freshly squeezed lemon juice
Rosemary sprigs (garnish)

Rosemary is actually a shrub, and if you've ever grown it, you know that it can grow quite tall. Lovers of the herb don't mind, of course. All the more to enjoy. The lovely name comes from the Latin for "dew of the sea." The herb has many positive associations in folklore. Placed under the pillow, it supposedly warded off nightmares. A love charm, it was carried in Greek wedding ceremonies. Frequently smelling rosemary supposedly kept one young, but a man indifferent to the smell would be incapable of true love.

Preheat oven to 500 degrees. Remove any gristle from lamb. Arrange in a single layer in the bottom of a large roasting pan. Sprinkle with rosemary, pepper, and garlic. Roast, uncovered, until meat is well browned, about 30 minutes. Stir in chopped onion, broth, and wine, scraping up and incorporating brown particles from pan. Reduce oven temperature to 375 degrees. Cover and bake one hour. Add mushrooms, onions, and carrots. Bake until vegetables are tender, about 40 minutes. (Add stock if liquid reduces too much.) Remove from oven. Remove meat and vegetables from pan and keep warm.

Skim fat from pan juices. Place pan on stove over high heat. Add cream to pan and boil, stirring constantly until sauce thickens. Remove from heat. Pour sauce onto warm serving plates, spoon lamb and vegetables on top, drizzle with lemon juice, and garnish with rosemary.

YIELD: 4 TO 6 SERVINGS

NOISETTES OF LAMB WITH SAUCE PERNOD

From that unmistakable landmark, the Hotel del Coronado, comes an unmistakably superb lamb entree, created by executive chef Jay Pastoral.

**2 lamb loins, about
½ pound each
Salt and freshly ground
pepper
2 ounces fresh spinach,
rinsed well, stems
removed
3 ounces butter**

Sauce:

**2 ounces Pernod
8 ounces beef broth
½ cup unsalted butter,
softened**

Butterfly loins and pound each, flattening to a half-inch thickness. Place the loins side to side, overlapping one inch. Pound the overlapping seam to make one piece. Season with salt and pepper.

Spread spinach leaves over the entire surface of the meat. Roll loin tightly and refrigerate one hour. Cut roll into eight even slices. Use toothpicks to secure slices.

Heat a large skillet over medium heat and add butter. Saute noisettes, about one minute each side. Remove from skillet and keep warm. Deglaze the skillet with Pernod, add broth, and simmer five minutes. Remove from heat and gradually stir in butter. Continue stirring until butter is well blended.

Lace sauce over noisettes on warm serving plates, or spoon sauce onto plates and top with noisettes.
Serve immediately.

YIELD: 4 SERVINGS

GRILLED LAMB CHOPS

½ cup chopped fresh mint
4 cloves garlic, crushed
2 cups dry sherry
3 pounds lamb chops,
  trimmed of fat

Combine mint, garlic, and sherry and pour over chops, covering all sides. Marinate several hours at room temperature, turning chops occasionally.

Grill over hot coals, basting with marinade, until meat is cooked.

YIELD: 4 TO 6 SERVINGS

GRILLED BUTTERFLY OF LAMB

This exotic combination of flavors will surprise those who aren't great lamb fanciers. For best flavor, marinate meat 24 hours.

1 leg of lamb, 4 to 6
  pounds, butterflied
1 cup Dijon mustard
2 cups soy sauce
2 cups peanut oil
3 cloves garlic, crushed

Have your butcher prepare the butterfly cut. Combine remaining ingredients, pour over meat to cover all surfaces. Cover and refrigerate 16 hours. Remove from refrigerator, turn meat, and marinate an additional 8 hours at room temperature.

Grill over hot coals, basting frequently, about 45 minutes to an hour.

YIELD: 8 SERVINGS

LAMB CURRY

Through trial and error ("the only way to learn how to cook"), David Nelson developed this recipe over the last fifteen years. Nelson writes the Restaurant and Society column for the *Los Angeles Times,* San Diego County Edition, and is frequently asked to prepare his special curry for dinner guests. Delicious, simple to prepare, and relatively inexpensive, this curry can easily be altered to taste, but a good quality curry powder is essential. Use it freely: "a fragrant curry is the best."

⅓ cup olive oil

2 teaspoons mustard seed

2 or 3 large onions, chopped

1 4-ounce piece of fresh ginger root, peeled and minced

3 cloves garlic

5 tablespoons curry powder (Indian preferred)

4 pounds lean lamb, cubed

½ teaspoon cayenne pepper

2 teaspoons salt

2 tablespoons vinegar

1 cup water

1 large apple, peeled, cored, and cubed

1 large banana, sliced

2 tablespoons mango chutney

1 tablespoon flaked coconut

1 cup heavy cream

Juice of 1 lime

Condiments: Chutneys, Indian pickles, sliced bananas in lemon juice, chopped cucumber and mint in plain yogurt, raisins, unsalted cashews or peanuts, coconut

Heat oil in a heavy pot and add mustard seed. Cover. Seeds will pop, sounding like popcorn. Add onion and saute until transparent. Add ginger, garlic, and curry powder and saute five minutes. Add all other ingredients except cream and lime juice. Simmer 2½ to 3 hours until meat is tender. Stir in cream, raise heat slightly (but be careful not to boil), and cook 15 minutes more, until sauce is thick and smooth. Turn off heat, stir in lime juice. If prepared in advance, add lime juice after reheating.

Serve with rice and offer condiments individually.

YIELD: 4 SERVINGS

MEDALLIONS OF LAMB WITH HORSERADISH AND CUCUMBER

Jack Huxtable, chef at Sheppard's Restaurant, notes that the sauce he created for these medallions also works well with any red meat—steaks, roasts, or chops. Ask your butcher to prepare medallions for you.

½ onion, diced
3 ounces white wine
3 ounces white wine vinegar
1 cup chicken stock or broth
1 cup heavy cream
Prepared horseradish, to taste
Salt and freshly ground pepper, to taste

2 tablespoons oil
1 lamb loin, boned, trimmed, cut into medallions
2 tablespoons unsalted butter
1 large cucumber, peeled, seeded, julienned
1 ripe tomato peeled, seeded, diced

Place onions in a saucepan and "sweat" them by cooking slowly over medium-low heat without browning. Add wine and vinegar, increase heat, and reduce the liquid by three-fourths. Add chicken stock and reduce by three-fourths. Add cream and reduce until sauce is thick. Do not boil. Add horseradish and seasonings. Strain. Sauce can be made in advance and reheated.

Heat oil in saute pan and saute lamb until medium-rare. Transfer to serving dishes. Wipe pan and melt butter. Saute cucumber for one minute. Add tomato. Remove from heat.

To serve, ladle the warm sauce around the lamb. Scatter the cucumber and tomato on top of the sauce.

YIELD: 4 SERVINGS

BARBECUE SAUCE

For slow cooking in the oven or for marinating and basting grilled meats, this is a traditional favorite. Breaking tradition is fun, though. Ever grill whole onions? They are wonderfully sweet when grilled—not like onions at all. Ever barbecue thick-sliced potatoes? Both go well with this sauce. Give 'em a try.

½ cup vinegar
1 clove garlic, crushed
2 tablespoons
  Worcestershire sauce
1 teaspoon dry mustard
2 tablespoons butter

1½ teaspoons Tabasco
  sauce
2 tablespoons sugar
1 cup catsup
Salt, to taste

Combine ingredients in a saucepan, mixing well. Simmer ten minutes.

Preheat oven to 275 degrees or prepare coals for grilling. To bake, brush meat with sauce and place in a shallow baking pan. Pour remaining sauce over the top and bake, basting occasionally, about two hours or until sauce begins to dry out. Serve. To grill, pour sauce over meat, covering all pieces, and let stand a few minutes. Place meat over medium-hot coals, prepared for a long, slow grilling. Grill (with a closed hood), turning meat and basting frequently.

YIELD: APPROXIMATELY 1½ CUPS

AMBER BARBECUE SAUCE

¼ cup oil
¾ cup chopped onion
¾ cup catsup
¾ cup water
⅓ cup lime juice
3 tablespoons sugar
3 tablespoons
  Worcestershire sauce

3 tablespoons prepared
  mustard
2 teaspoons salt
½ teaspoon freshly ground
  pepper

Heat skillet and add oil. Saute onions over medium heat until tender. Combine remaining ingredients and add to onions in skillet. Cover and simmer one hour, stirring occasionally.

YIELD: APPROXIMATELY 2 CUPS

TARRAGON MAYONNAISE FOR MARINATED BEEF

This flavorful garnish for beef may also find itself spread between slices of sourdough bread for sandwiches. Try it on grilled swordfish or in chicken salad as well. Recipe can easily be increased proportionally—use a blender or food processor to make large quantities.

2 egg yolks
Salt and freshly ground
  pepper, to taste
2 tablespoons tarragon
  vinegar
1 cup olive oil
1 tablespoon lemon juice
2 teaspoons Worcestershire
  sauce
1 clove garlic, minced
1 teaspoon minced onion
1 teaspoon finely chopped
  fresh parsley
Pinch tarragon

Whisk together yolks, salt, pepper, and half the vinegar. Slowly whisk in half the oil in a very thin stream. Add remaining vinegar, lemon juice, and Worcestershire sauce. Blend thoroughly. Whisk in remaining oil gradually. Check seasoning.

Add garlic, onion, parsley, and tarragon, mixing well. Store in glass container in the refrigerator until serving. Flavor improves if allowed to mellow several hours or overnight.

YIELD: APPROXIMATELY 1½ CUPS

SAVORY CHOUCROUTE

Choucroute tastes best if prepared a day ahead and reheated before serving. Purchase sauerkraut packed in refrigerated jars rather than the canned variety.

2 pounds sauerkraut
½ pound slab bacon
4 tablespoons unsalted
  butter
¾ cup julienned carrots
1½ cups sliced onions
5 sprigs parsley
7 peppercorns
2 bay leaves

½ cup gin
1 cup dry white wine
1 cup chicken stock
2 cups beef stock, or more
  if needed
Salt, to taste
1 pound knockwurst
1 pound bratwurst

Pour off brine from sauerkraut and rinse. Drain and repeat. Squeeze out all water. Cut bacon into pieces and cook in one cup water, simmering about 10 minutes. Drain. Melt butter in a three-quart, non-aluminum casserole over medium heat. Add bacon, carrots, and onions and cook slowly for 10 minutes. Mix in sauerkraut and cook an additional 10 minutes. Add parsley, peppercorns, bay leaves, gin, wine, and stock. Mix well and add salt.

Preheat oven to 300 degrees. Butter a piece of waxed paper large enough to cover kraut. Place buttered side down in pan and press. Bring to a simmer, cover, and bake in the oven 4½ hours.

Prick sausages and brown lightly in a skillet. Remove cover and waxed paper from casserole and add sausages to kraut (without rendered fat). Continue oven cooking for another 30 minutes or until liquid is absorbed.

YIELD: 6 SERVINGS

SAUSAGE STUFFED PEPPERS

1½ pounds spicy Italian
  sausage
1 onion, chopped
2 cloves garlic, minced
1 eggplant, peeled and
  cubed
1 ripe tomato, chopped
¼ pound mushrooms,
  coarsely chopped

1 teaspoon each dried
  thyme, cumin, crushed
  fennel
8 large red sweet peppers
½ cup chopped walnuts
1 egg, lightly beaten
1 cup shredded Mozzarella
  cheese

*Oriental eggplants are
smaller and straighter than
their American counterparts.
They can be used in any
eggplant recipe and do not
need to be peeled or salted,
if fresh. These delicate
vegetables are delicious
grilled whole.*

Remove sausage casings and crumble meat into a skillet
over medium heat. Saute until browned. Drain off excess
fat. Add onion, and garlic and saute until tender. Stir in
eggplant, tomato, mushrooms, thyme, cumin, and fennel.
Check seasonings and add additional spices to taste, as
desired. Cook uncovered, stirring occasionally, until
eggplant is tender and liquid has evaporated, about
15 minutes. Remove from heat.

Cut tops off peppers and reserve. Scrape out seeds and
veins. Drop peppers into a pot of rapidly boiling water.
Boil uncovered two to three minutes. Douse immediately
in cold water. Drain.

Preheat oven to 400 degrees. Stir walnuts, egg, and half of
the cheese into eggplant mixture. Spoon mixture into
peppers in even portions. Replace tops. Place peppers in a
shallow, buttered baking dish. Cover and bake 25 minutes.
Uncover, remove tops, sprinkle with remaining cheese,
and bake an additional 10 minutes, or until cheese is
melted and bubbly.

YIELD: 8 SERVINGS

BEEF STIR FRY WITH BROCCOLI AND OYSTER SAUCE

1 pound filet mignon,
  sliced very thin
2 tablespoons cornstarch
1 tablespoon soy sauce
1 teaspoon sugar
½ tablespoon peanut oil
4 tablespoons oyster sauce
½ cup water
3 garlic cloves, minced
1 tablespoon grated ginger
  root
Peanut oil for frying
1 head broccoli, cut into
  florets
½ cup chicken stock

Mix together beef, one tablespoon cornstarch, soy sauce, sugar, and peanut oil. Set aside. Combine oyster sauce, water, remaining cornstarch, garlic, and ginger. Set aside.

Heat two tablespoons peanut oil in a hot wok until oil barely begins to smoke. Add meat mixture and toss fry briefly until meat changes color. Remove meat from wok. Heat an additional two tablespoons of oil in the same manner. Add broccoli, toss to coat with oil, and add stock. Cover and simmer briefly until broccoli is just tender.

Return meat to wok and toss with broccoli. Add oyster sauce mixture, toss to coat all pieces, and allow sauce to thicken. Place on warm platter and serve immediately.

YIELD: 2 TO 4 SERVINGS

GRILLED CARNE ASADA

1½-pound flank or
  skirt steak
½ tablespoon coarse salt
1 teaspoon ground cumin
1 teaspoon oregano
¼ teaspoon ground cloves
1 bay leaf, crumbled
1 clove garlic, mashed
Juice of 1 lemon
Juice of 1 orange
12 corn or flour tortillas
Salsa, guacamole, chopped
  cilantro, shredded Jack
  cheese (garnish)

Trim any fat from meat. In a small bowl, combine salt, cumin, oregano, cloves, and bay leaf. Rub mixture into both sides of steak. Rub in garlic. Pound meat, working seasonings into meat. Place meat in a shallow dish, squeeze juices over both sides, and refrigerate two to four hours.

Bring meat to room temperature. Prepare coals. Grill meat over medium coals, about six minutes each side, or until well done. Remove from grill, allow to settle a few minutes, and slice thinly across the grain. Serve on warm tortillas and garnish as desired.

YIELD: 4 TO 6 SERVINGS

BEEF STEW WITH SALSA

Delicious with Mexican spoon bread. (See recipe on page 41.)

¼ cup olive oil
1 onion, finely chopped
2 cloves garlic, minced
2 ripe tomatoes, peeled and coarsely chopped
2 pounds lean beef, cubed
¼ cup red wine vinegar
¾ cup tomato puree
1 cup dry red wine
1 tablespoon chopped cilantro
2 tablespoons chopped fresh parsley
1 bay leaf
1 tablespoon chopped fresh oregano
7 ounces green chili salsa
Salt and freshly ground pepper, to taste
¼ cup grated Jack cheese
Cilantro sprigs (garnish)

Heat a large skillet and add two tablespoons olive oil. Saute onion and garlic over medium heat until tender. Remove with a slotted spoon and set aside. Add tomatoes to skillet and saute three to five minutes. Pour tomatoes and pan juices into a bowl and set aside.

Heat remaining oil and saute beef until browned. Return onion and garlic to pan and stir. Add tomatoes and remaining ingredients, except cheese. Bring the mixture to a boil, stirring frequently, reduce heat, cover and simmer 90 minutes. Remove cover and simmer an additional 15 to 30 minutes or until stew thickens. Pour into warm serving bowls, top with cheese, and garnish with cilantro.

YIELD: 4 SERVINGS

M. GRANT'S CHILI NO. XIV

We wonder what Michael Grant's Chili No. XIII tastes like, or all the others. Perhaps he'll reveal this chili evolution in his *San Diego Union* column.

4 pounds chuck roast
4 pounds pork roast
3 tablespoons whole cumin seed
2 green peppers
1 sweet red pepper
3 Anaheim chilies
2 fresh jalapenos

28 ounces tomatoes, with juice
3 medium onions, minced
5 cloves garlic, minced
1 tablespoon dried oregano
2 tablespoons salt
Freshly ground pepper, to taste
Water, to cover

Buy inexpensive chuck and pork roasts. Have your butcher trim off excess fat and grind the cuts in a coarse "chili grind."

Toast cumin seed in a dry skillet until golden and fragrant. Use mortar and pestle to crush seeds, or grind them to a powder in a coffee grinder.

Roast peppers and chilies under broiler or over gas flames to blacken skins. Place in a tightly closed grocery sack and allow to steam for five minutes. Peel off skins and remove seeds. Puree with tomatoes in a food processor or blender.

In a large pot, cook ground meat in its own juices a pound at a time until meat is gray. Remove meat and cook onions and garlic in the juices until onions are transparent. Return meat to pot and add tomato-pepper puree and all seasonings. Add water to cover. Simmer, covered, for two hours or longer, stirring occasionally. Skim off surface fat before serving.

YIELD: APPROXIMATELY 18 SERVINGS

CALIFORNIA PIZZA

Unbelievably good—just like the weather.

Dough:

1 cup lukewarm water
  (110 degrees)
2 packages yeast
3½ cups unbleached flour
1 teaspoon coarse salt
1 teaspoon sugar
1 tablespoon olive oil

Pesto:

1 cup olive oil
2 cups fresh basil leaves
2 cloves garlic, chopped
3 tablespoons pine nuts
½ cup freshly grated
  Parmesan cheese

1 onion, thinly sliced
1 sweet red pepper, seeded
  and sliced into strips
1 green pepper, seeded and
  sliced into strips
2 tablespoons olive oil
1 tablespoon water
½ pound garlic and fennel
  sausage or sweet Italian
  sausage
3 ounces goat cheese
10 ounces Mozzarella
  cheese, coarsely grated
2 tablespoons freshly grated
  Parmesan cheese
2 teaspoons cornmeal

Prepare dough: Dissolve yeast in water and set aside. Mix flour, salt, and sugar in a bowl. Make a "well" in the center, pour in yeast solution and olive oil. Blend in the flour using a fork, working toward the outside of the well. As dough becomes stiff, incorporate remaining flour by hand. Gather into a ball and knead eight to ten minutes on a floured board. Place in an oil-coated bowl, cover with a damp cloth, and let rise in a warm, draft-free place until doubled in size, approximately two hours.

Prepare pesto sauce using a blender or food processor. Combine all ingredients except cheese. Process but do not create a puree. Stir in cheese. Set aside.

Saute onions and peppers in one tablespoon olive oil and water in a large skillet over medium heat. Stir frequently until peppers are soft. Drain and set aside. Brown sausage, breaking into pieces as it cooks. Drain off excess fat. Chop coarsely and set aside.

Preheat oven to 400 degrees. Spread remaining olive oil evenly over a 12-inch pizza pan. Sprinkle with cornmeal. Punch down pizza dough, flatten lightly with a rolling pin, turn and flatten with fingers. Place dough in pan and spread to edges with fingertips. Bake five minutes.

Spread pesto sauce over dough. Crumble goat cheese evenly over pesto. Add onions and peppers, sausage, and cheeses. Bake 10 minutes or until crust is slightly brown and cheese is bubbly.

CHILES RELLENOS GUADALAJARA

Cooked and shredded meat can be added to the chilies for variation. Cook meat with chorizo for added flavor, but drain off the rendered fat.

1½ pounds ripe tomatoes,
   peeled
1 onion, cut into chunks
½ stick cinnamon,
   crumbled
3 tablespoons peanut oil
Salt and freshly ground
   pepper, to taste
6 fresh green chilies, peeled
½ pound Jack cheese,
   cut into 6 strips
3 eggs, separated
Flour, to coat
2 tablespoons unsalted
   butter
½ cup chicken stock

Preheat oven to 350 degrees. Puree tomatoes, onion, and cinnamon in a blender or food processor. Simmer mixture in one tablespoon oil over medium heat until thickened. Add salt and pepper to taste. Set aside.

Slit chilies on one side and remove seeds. Insert one strip of cheese in each and secure with toothpick. Beat egg whites until stiff. In a separate bowl, beat egg yolks and fold into whites. Roll chilies in flour to coat and dip in egg batter. Heat butter and two tablespoons oil in a large skillet over medium-high heat. Fry chilies until puffy and browned. Pour chicken stock into a shallow baking pan and add fried chilies. Add sauce, cover, and bake 30 minutes.

YIELD: 3 OR 6 SERVINGS

Sweet Finishes

STRAWBERRIES AND CREME FRAICHE

½ cup heavy cream
¼ cup sugar
½ teaspoon almond extract
½ cup sour cream
2 pints strawberries
Fresh mint sprigs (garnish)

In a chilled bowl, beat together cream, sugar, and almond extract until stiff. Fold in sour cream until evenly blended.

Wash and hull strawberries. Toss gently in cream mixture and refrigerate. To serve, spoon berries into champagne or sherbet glasses and top each with extra creme fraiche and a sprig of mint.

YIELD: 6 SERVINGS

RASPBERRY MOUSSE

1 cup sour cream
1¼ cups ripe raspberries
1 cup sugar
1 teaspoon vanilla extract
Kiwi slices (garnish)

Blend all ingredients together until smooth and well combined. Pour into a small loaf pan or into a decorative mold or souffle dish suitable for freezing. Cover and freeze until firm, at least four hours or overnight.

To serve, unmold and slice. Top with kiwi.

YIELD: 6 SERVINGS

Fresh fruit dipped in melted chocolate or caramel sauce is an elegant finish for more formal fare. A caramel sauce we prefer is easy to prepare and keep warm. Melt ½ cup sweet butter and 14 ounces of caramels in a heavy saucepan. Stir in ¼ cup finely chopped pecans, 1 tablespoon milk, and ¼ teaspoon rum extract. Stir vigorously. Dip fruit—apples, pears, strawberries, or pineapple, for example—using wooden skewers.

MARINATED BERRIES

We've chosen three berry types for this recipe, but any number of fresh varieties can be combined successfully.

½ cup sugar
½ cup water
½ cup good-quality
  Burgundy
½ teaspoon cinnamon
1 tablespoon lemon juice
1 pint fresh raspberries
1 pint fresh blueberries
1 pint fresh blackberries

When selecting berries, choose packages that show no seepage on the bottom. The fruit should have no blemishes or mold. Blackberries should be shiny and very dark; berries with any light or red drupelets will be sour. Raspberries should not be shiny, however. Stems should always be absent and the berries should be even in color. Loganberries, when available, are a wonderful choice. They are the best of raspberries and blackberries but have none of the tiny "seeds."

Bring sugar and water to a boil, reduce heat and stir until sugar is dissolved. Remove from heat and add wine, cinnamon, and lemon juice. Cool.

Wash berries and drain thoroughly. Pour liquid over berries and marinate at least two hours. Chill slightly before serving in parfait glasses or stemmed dessert goblets.

YIELD: 8 TO 10 SERVINGS

FRESH PEACH ICE CREAM

3 cups peach pulp and juice
Juice of 1 large orange
Juice of 3 lemons
3 cups sugar

1 teaspoon vanilla extract
1 quart milk
1 pint cream

Mix together peach pulp, all juices, sugar, and vanilla. Let stand at room temperature three hours. Mix with milk and cream and pour into an ice cream maker. Freeze.

YIELD: 10 TO 12 SERVINGS OR 1 GALLON

IRISH COFFEE SHAKE

This recipe calls for coffee ice cream, which can easily be replaced by a good quality vanilla ice cream mixed with a teaspoon of instant coffee. Either way, the result makes slurping hard to resist.

½ cup milk
¼ cup whiskey
1 quart coffee ice cream

1 teaspoon instant espresso
Heavy cream, whipped
4 cinnamon sticks

Combine milk, whiskey, ice cream, and coffee in a blender or food processor. Blend just until well combined. Pour into mugs, top with whipped cream, and insert a cinnamon stick in each.

YIELD: 4 SERVINGS

CHOCOLATE FRAMBOISE ICE CREAM

Raspberries and chocolate combine in this frozen dessert to a rapturous result. An ice cream freezer isn't required to make this, although one can be used.

**5 ounces semisweet or
  bittersweet chocolate
1¼ cups milk
8 egg yolks
1 cup sugar
⅓ cup framboise liqueur
2 cups whipping cream
Fresh raspberries (topping)**

Combine chocolate and milk in a saucepan over medium heat. Stir constantly until chocolate melts, but do not boil. In a separate heavy saucepan, beat egg yolks with sugar until they are light in color. Add chocolate mixture slowly, beating constantly over low heat until thickened. Remove from heat and add the liqueur.

Refrigerate until completely chilled. Whip cream until soft peaks form. Fold into the chocolate "custard." Freeze in an ice cream freezer or pour into a glass bowl and freeze.

To serve, spoon ice cream into dessert goblets. Top with fresh, ripe raspberries. For variation, substitute Grand Marnier and two tablespoons instant coffee or Kahlua and ¼ teaspoon cinnamon.

YIELD: 6 SERVINGS OR 1 QUART

GREAT-GRANDMOTHER'S COOKED ICE CREAM

She knew a good thing or two. Leftover "cooked" ice cream doesn't form ice crystals in the freezer, but leftovers are rare. This recipe is an excellent basis for many variations. Fruit, peppermint, vanilla, or chocolate chips can be added to the cream mixture during the freezing process.

12 ounces evaporated milk
1 quart half and half
½ cup milk
4 eggs
2½ cups sugar
1 pint whipping cream

Combine first three ingredients and warm over low heat. Separate eggs. Mix yolks with sugar and add to milk mixture. Cook, stirring constantly, until thickened. Remove from heat to cool, then refrigerate. Whip cream. In a separate bowl, beat egg whites until light. Fold whipped cream and egg whites into mixture until well blended. Freeze in an ice cream freezer. (Add flavoring part way through process, before cream completely hardens.)

YIELD: 10 TO 12 SERVINGS OR 1 GALLON

ICE CREAM PIE WITH BUTTER CRUNCH CRUST

Vanilla ice cream is the choice here, but others work well, such as pralines and cream. Slice pie and drizzle with a warm fudge topping or butterscotch sauce.

**½ cup unsalted butter,
  softened**
¼ cup brown sugar, packed
1 cup flour
½ cup chopped walnuts
1 quart vanilla ice cream

*The darker the brown sugar,
the more cane molasses it
contains and the "deeper"
the flavor.*

Preheat oven to 400 degrees. Mix together butter, sugar, flour, and walnuts in a medium bowl until well blended. Spread loosely into the bottom of a baking pan (13 x 9 inches) and bake 15 minutes. To form crust, reserve ¾ cup and press remaining mixture into the bottom and sides of a nine-inch pie pan. When completely cool, fill with ice cream, sprinkle with reserve crust mixture and freeze at least one hour.

YIELD: 8 SERVINGS

CHOCOLATE CHIP PIE

Delicious right out of the oven, this pie is best served
warm. Top with whipped cream or ice cream, as desired.

2 eggs
1 cup sugar
½ cup flour
½ cup unsalted butter,
  melted and cooled
1 teaspoon vanilla extract
1 cup broken pecans
  (or walnuts, almonds)
6 ounces semisweet
  chocolate chips
1 unbaked pie shell,
  nine inches

Preheat oven to 350 degrees. Beat eggs slightly, add sugar,
and blend thoroughly. Add flour, butter, and vanilla,
blending each addition well. Add nuts and chocolate chips.
Pour mixture into pie shell and bake one hour.

YIELD: 6 SERVINGS

PEACH PIE

Served warm or cold, this is an all-time, old-time favorite.

Double crust pie pastry
1 egg white
**5 cups peaches, peeled and
  sliced**
¾ cup sugar
⅓ cup flour
**1 tablespoon freshly
  squeezed lemon juice**
**½ teaspoon grated lemon
  rind**
**½ teaspoon ground
  cinnamon**

Preheat oven to 425 degrees. Prepare pastry dough and roll out half. Line a buttered nine-inch pan and brush dough with egg white.

Combine remaining ingredients in a bowl and set aside. Roll out remaining dough. Pour peach mixture into pie pan and top with dough. Slit top and trim sides.

Bake 45 minutes to one hour or until crust is golden.

YIELD: 6 SERVINGS

FRESH BLUEBERRY PIE

1 cup sugar
3 tablespoons cornstarch
1 cup water
4 cups fresh blueberries,
  rinsed and drained
1 tablespoon freshly
  squeezed lemon juice
2 tablespoons unsalted
  butter
1 prebaked pie shell,
  nine inches
Heavy cream, whipped
  (topping)

Mix sugar, cornstarch, and water in a saucepan over low heat. Stir constantly until mixture begins to thicken. Add half the blueberries, stirring constantly. When mixture becomes very thick, add lemon juice and butter. Stir until butter melts, remove from heat, and cool to room temperature. Stir in the remaining blueberries. Refrigerate until ready to serve. To serve, fill pie shell with blueberry mixture. Top slices with lightly whipped cream.

YIELD: 6 TO 8 SERVINGS

ORANGE CREAM MASCARPONE

Mascarpone, a double-cream cheese, could be described as similar to a buttery Devonshire cream. We've combined it with the flavor of oranges, but it is also delicious with other fruits and quality brandies.

4 egg yolks
½ cup sugar
8 ounces mascarpone
4 tablespoons orange
  liqueur (Grand Marnier)
1 orange, peeled and sliced
  (garnish)

Orange liqueurs include Cointreau, Grand Marnier, Curacao, and Triple Sec, with Grand Marnier generally the preferred choice for dessert making. Mandarine Napoleon, a tangerine liqueur, is similar and works well as a substitute.

Beat together yolks and sugar until thick and pale. Add the cheese and beat until completely mixed in. Add two tablespoons liqueur and beat again. Refrigerate two or three hours. Toss orange slices in remaining liqueur and set aside until ready to serve.

Spoon mascarpone into stemmed dessert goblets. Top with orange slices.

YIELD: 4 SERVINGS

ALMOND TART

Crust:

1 cup flour
1½ tablespoons sugar
½ cup unsalted butter, cold
1 tablespoon cold water
½ teaspoon vanilla extract
¼ teaspoon almond extract

Filling:

1 cup sugar
1 cup sliced almonds
¾ cup heavy cream
2 teaspoons Amaretto
2 drops almond extract
Heavy cream, whipped
    (topping)

To prepare crust, mix flour and sugar, and cut butter into mixture until it forms coarse crumbs. Work in the water and extracts to form a stiff dough. (Add additional drops of water if needed.) Press dough into a buttered tart pan with removable bottom. Cover with plastic wrap and refrigerate at least one hour. (Can be prepared ahead and refrigerated overnight.)

Preheat oven to 400 degrees. Combine filling ingredients in a bowl and let stand until sugar dissolves, about 25 minutes.

Bake crust 10 minutes or until golden. (Fill shell with pie weights or, halfway through baking, push sides back into place with a wine cork.) Remove from oven and reduce oven temperature to 350 degrees. Pour filling into crust. Bake on a baking sheet (to catch drips) 25 minutes or until evenly brown and caramelized. Cool to room temperature and remove from pan. Serve at room temperature topped with fresh, whipped cream.

YIELD: 8 SERVINGS

Almonds, golden California walnuts, and pistachios are three very popular nuts grown in our sunny state. Most almonds eaten in this country are grown in California. Store nuts, which won't be eaten out of hand or used in cooking right away, in airtight containers in the freezer. They can be frozen shelled or unshelled. Unshelled nuts can be used directly from the freezer without thawing.

RASPBERRY MARZIPAN TART

Pastry:

1 ¼ cups flour
⅓ cup sugar
1 teaspoon baking powder
½ cup unsalted butter,
  softened
1 egg beaten

¼ cup raspberry preserves

Glaze:

½ cup powdered sugar
2 to 3 teaspoons lemon
  juice

Filling:

⅔ cup sugar
½ cup unsalted butter,
  softened
½ teaspoon almond extract
2 eggs
1 cup almonds, finely
  chopped
⅓ cup raspberry preserves

Sugared almonds are a sweet treat. Cook 1 cup sugar, 1 teaspoon cinnamon, 1 teaspoon vanilla extract, and 3 tablespoons very strong coffee (brewed), stirring until very thick. Remove from heat and stir in 2 cups whole toasted blanched almonds. Cool on waxed paper.

Preheat oven to 350 degrees. Blend pastry ingredients (except raspberry preserves) with pastry cutter or knives until a dough forms. Press dough into bottom and sides of a buttered nine-inch tart pan with a removable bottom. Spread with ¼ cup preserves and refrigerate.

Cream sugar, butter, and almond extract until light and fluffy. Add eggs one at a time, beating well after each. Stir in almonds. Add filling to tart pan and spread evenly.

Bake 40 to 50 minutes or until golden brown. Cool two hours. Loosen pastry edges with a sharp knife and gently remove tart from pan. Spread the filling with ⅓ cup preserves.

Blend together powdered sugar and lemon until smooth. Drizzle glaze over tart filling. Refrigerate. Bring to room temperature before serving.

YIELD: 10 SERVINGS

Fresh Fruit

*F*ruit is an odd word, as are some of the words associated with it—peel, pit, pulp, pith, rind. Yet one bite of a ripe apricot, fresh from the tree, and fruity words become descriptively transcendental—succulent, saporous, ambrosial, delectable. Such pleasures of Eden are not forbidden in sunny California. We are fortunate to have homegrown fresh fruit available most of the year, even more fortunate to have a wide selection that includes unusual varieties.

This heavenly abundance is particularly welcome to those who love fresh fruit desserts. Fruit pies and tarts, fruit-filled pastries, and poached fruit are classics, but even uncooked berries or sliced fruit, drizzled with liqueur or glazed, or added as a topping to ice cream or a genoise, are equally delicious and beautiful. For any of these desserts to please the palate as much as the eye, the fruit must be very fresh, of good quality, and quite ripe.

Tests for ripeness vary as much as the selection. A ripe cantaloupe gives slightly to gentle pressure, is lightly fragrant and has a firm, yellow skin. Peak season for California cantaloupes, the finest, is long, from June through November. Honeydews peak in August through October, and when ripe, are one of the sweetest fruits of all. California honeydews are said to be the best. Skins should be a creamy butter color and feel like velvet. They do not ripen off the vine, so avoid selecting hard melons lacking fragrance. Watermelons can't be tested for ripeness, according to one expert, until they are cut open. A dark red color and firm flesh indicates a fruit with sweetness and flavor. Watermelons and cantaloupes can be stored uncut at room temperature, but honeydews should be refrigerated once purchased.

California is known for its citrus fruit—oranges, tangelos, grapefruit, tangerines, lemons, limes. California Valencia oranges arrive in the markets from May through December and navel oranges are in season from November to June. These varieties are said to be best when they've been in season for a few months. For any citrus fruit, color and size are not the best indications of quality. Instead, one should select fruit based on the thinness of skin and the weight in relation to size.

In addition to citrus fruits, much more comes fresh to market from California growers. Peaches, apricots, plums, figs, melons, cherries, and nectarines are but a few fruits of the annual harvest. Grapes, both table and wine, are the state's most valuable fruit. More than ninety percent of the table grapes consumed in the country are grown on California vines. Ideal soil and climate also make California strawberries a delightful possibility nearly all year. More strawberries are grown here than any place in the world, over seventy-five percent of the nation's crop.

For desserts, strawberries are traditionally featured in shortcakes, tarts, and that all-time favorite, fresh strawberry ice cream. Lovers of the color and taste, however, also combine these characteristics with other fruits for variation. Slice or pureed strawberries served with ripe kiwi fruit makes an absolutely beautiful dessert. The kiwi, once exotic, is now common. When sliced, kiwi doesn't discolor, an advantage when preparing a dessert in advance. And despite its delicate color and texture, the tart-sweet flavor isn't lost, even when sliced or pureed. The popular acceptance of this fruit has given growers and fruit lovers the incentive to try other exotics, such as the carambola or star fruit, which possesses a flavor combining the best of plums and sweet grapes with a hint of citrus, or the cherimoya, also called custard apple for its creamy texture. These are intriguing dessert fare, whether served alone or with other fruits, or served with a fresh berry puree topping.

Two other uncommon fruits grown in California are becoming more available—Asian pears and blood oranges—and each is ideal for dessert preparation. Asian pears are very juicy and have a refreshing, light sweet taste. Chilled and sliced, they are elegant dipped in an apricot or blackberry sauce, or good company to fruit sorbets. The flesh of a blood orange is a brilliant color, a dark, cherry red, and has an intensely citrus flavor with raspberry overtones. They are often seedless, making them ideal for compotes or fresh fruit tarts.

The cool, smooth taste of sliced melon, the aroma of a peeled tangerine, the visual perfection of a fresh, ripe strawberry—fruit pleases the senses, whether it adds zest, a touch of sweetness, or shines alone. In its many varieties, each unique in shape, color, and flavor, it also adds a richness to the vocabulary of foods.

◆

TART APPLE PUDDING WITH DATES AND PECANS

Wonderfully rich and served warm with a sweet cream topping.

½ cup flour
1 teaspoon baking powder
2 eggs
¾ cup brown sugar
1 cup tart apples, peeled
  and diced
½ cup finely chopped dates
½ cup chopped pecans
  (or walnuts)

Topping:

½ cup cream
½ cup butter
¾ cup sugar
1 teaspoon vanilla extract

Preheat oven to 325 degrees. Butter and flour a baking pan (8 x 8 inches).

Sift together flour and baking powder. Set aside. Beat eggs and add sugar, beating constantly. Fold in flour. Add apples, dates, and nuts. Pour into baking pan and bake 40 minutes.

As the pudding bakes, prepare topping. Combine topping ingredients and heat until butter melts and sugar is dissolved, stirring constantly. Do not boil. Keep warm.

Remove pudding from oven and allow to cool slightly. Pour a small pool of sauce onto serving dishes. Scoop a portion of pudding on top and drizzle with remaining sauce.

YIELD: 6 TO 8 SERVINGS

Jonathan apples are excellent for cooking, but may be hard to find. Pippin, Empire, Rome Beauty, McIntosh, and Granny Smith are varieties that work well in baking and in sauces. Often the less perfect an apple looks in color and shape, the better the taste. Apples should be hard, sound hollow when thumped, and the skin should fit very tightly. A pinkish blush on green or yellow apples indicates sweetness.

IMPERIAL COOKIES

These fragile cookies literally melt in your mouth.

1 cup unsalted butter,
  softened
¾ cup sugar
½ teaspoon baking soda
½ teaspoon vinegar
½ teaspoon vanilla extract
1½ cups flour
½ cup chopped nuts

Peanut butter cookies can be made without flour. Here's how: Combine two beaten eggs, 2 cups chunky peanut butter, 2 cups sugar, and 1 teaspoon vanilla extract. Roll into walnut-size balls and bake 10 minutes at 350 degrees.

Preheat oven to 300 degrees. Beat together butter, sugar, soda, vinegar, and vanilla with an electric mixer on high speed for 15 minutes. Fold in flour and nuts. Drop dough by the teaspoonful onto ungreased cookie sheets and bake 20 to 25 minutes.

YIELD: 3 DOZEN

MINIATURE CHEESECAKES

3 8-ounce packages cream
  cheese, softened
5 eggs
1½ teaspoons vanilla
1 cup sugar

Topping:

½ pint sour cream
¼ cup sugar
¼ teaspoon vanilla extract
Fresh fruit slices, pecan or
  walnut halves (garnish)

Preheat oven to 300 degrees. Line two muffin tins (for a dozen muffins each) with decorative paper liners.

Beat cream cheese until smooth. Add eggs one at a time, beating well with each addition. Add vanilla and gradually add sugar, blending well. (A food processor or blender works well.)

Distribute cream cheese mixture evenly among muffin cups. Bake 30 to 45 minutes or until lightly browned and cracks form on tops. Remove from oven and cool five minutes.

Blend together topping mixture. Spoon topping over each cake and bake five minutes more. Remove from oven and cool to room temperature. Remove individual cakes and freeze. To serve, allow cakes to stand at room temperature at least 15 minutes. Top each cake with fruit slices or nuts.

YIELD: 24 CHEESECAKES

CHEESECAKE

Some of us are convinced that cheesecake is the real ambrosia. This heavenly version can be elegantly garnished with mint sprigs, bittersweet chocolate leaves, or fresh fruit. Like most baked cheesecakes, it should be made a day or two in advance of serving.

Crust:

1¼ cups graham cracker crumbs
¼ cup granulated sugar
¼ cup unsalted butter, softened

Topping:

1 pint sour cream
½ cup sugar
½ teaspoon vanilla extract
½ teaspoon freshly squeezed lemon juice

Filling:

4 8-ounce packages cream cheese, softened
4 large eggs
1 cup sugar
1 teaspoon freshly squeezed lemon juice
1 teaspoon vanilla extract

Zwieback bread crumbs are an excellent substitute for cheesecake's traditional graham cracker crumb crust. Crush enough zwieback to yield a cup and a half of crumbs. Blend with a dash of salt, ¼ cup sweet butter, and ⅓ cup sugar. Press into a buttered pan and bake 10 minutes at 300 degrees. Cool and fill with cheesecake batter and bake according to recipe directions.

Preheat oven to 375 degrees. Combine crust ingredients and blend with fork or pastry knife. Press into the bottom and halfway up the sides of a ten-inch springform pan. Bake eight minutes. Remove from oven to cool.

Reduce oven temperature to 350 degrees. Combine all filling ingredients in a blender or food processor and blend until smooth. Pour into cooled crust and bake 50 to 55 minutes. Prepare topping before cheesecake finishes baking. Combine all topping ingredients and blend until well mixed. Pour over cheesecake immediately from the oven. Bake five to seven minutes more. Remove from oven. Cool completely, cover, and refrigerate overnight.

YIELD: 12 SERVINGS

KAHLUA CHEESECAKE

20 round chocolate wafers,
   crushed (1¼ cups)
⅓ cup unsalted butter,
   melted
16 ounces cream cheese,
   softened
2 eggs
½ cup sugar
2 tablespoons Kahlua

Topping:

2 tablespoons sugar
½ pint sour cream
1½ tablespoons Kahlua
Freshly ground nutmeg

Preheat oven to 350 degrees. Mix together crushed wafers and butter. Press into a nine-inch pie pan. Chill.

Blend cream cheese, eggs, sugar, and Kahlua until thoroughly combined. Pour into prepared crust and bake 15 to 20 minutes. Remove from oven and allow to cool at least 20 minutes before preparing topping.

Blend together all topping ingredients. Pour over cheesecake and bake five minutes. Remove from oven to cool. Cover and refrigerate at least overnight or up to two days. Garnish with nutmeg before serving.

YIELD: 8 SERVINGS

A fantastic finish for a Mexican feast is flaming papaya. Pour warm tequila over papaya slices and ignite. When flame dies down, serve slices over vanilla ice cream.

CHOCOLATE CHEESECAKE

Crust:

1½ cups graham cracker
   crumbs
⅓ cup sugar
½ cup unsalted butter,
   melted

Topping:

½ cup sour cream
1 tablespoon sugar
1½ teaspoons vanilla extract

Filling:

16 ounces cream cheese,
   room temperature
½ cup sugar
2 eggs
2 tablespoons freshly
   squeezed orange juice
1 tablespoon sour cream
1 teaspoon vanilla extract
1½ ounces unsweetened
   baking chocolate, melted

Chocolate leaves are elegant dessert garnishes. Wash and dry fresh green camellia or lemon leaves. Melt chocolate (not much will be needed) and brush onto the underside of each leaf in a thin, even layer. Place on a plate, chocolate side up, in the refrigerator for a few minutes until the chocolate has set. Gently peel away the leaf. Handle as little as possible.

Preheat oven to 350 degrees. Combine graham cracker crumbs, sugar, and butter. Mix well. Press into the bottom and sides of a nine-inch springform pan. Refrigerate.

Beat cream cheese until smooth and blend in sugar. Add eggs one at a time, beating well after each. Blend in orange juice, sour cream, and vanilla. Stir a heaping tablespoon of this mixture into the melted chocolate, then add chocolate to cream cheese mixture, blending well. Pour into crust and bake 45 minutes. Remove from oven to cool.

Combine topping ingredients and mix well. Spread over cheesecake and bake 15 minutes more. Remove from oven to cool. Refrigerate until ready to serve.

YIELD: 10 SERVINGS

CHOCOLATE PECAN TART

La Jolla's highly acclaimed restaurant, Gustaf Anders, provides this utterly delicious dessert recipe. Serve with a knife—it's dense and rich.

Chocolate Glaze:

8 ounces bittersweet
  chocolate
12 ounces raw cream
1 ounce unsalted butter

Tart:

4 ounces unsalted butter
4 ounces sugar
2 tablespoons raw cream
2 tablespoons flour
1 12-inch tart shell,
  partially baked
Pecan halves, enough to
  cover bottom of shell

To prepare glaze: Melt chocolate with cream over low heat, stirring often. Cool slightly, stir in butter, remove from heat, and set aside to cool.

Preheat oven to 375 degrees. In a saucepan, melt butter over low heat and add sugar, cream, and flour, stirring constantly. Add the pecan halves to this mixture, turning to coat them completely. Pour mixture into shell and spread to cover. Bake for 20 to 25 minutes or until mixture is caramelized. Remove from oven and cool completely. Pour and spread glaze over the top and refrigerate until solid.

YIELD: APPROXIMATELY 6 SERVINGS

Volumes have been written about chocolate—a subject and taste that's a passion for many. We like the way it's described by those who love it: lilting, well rounded, rich, mellow, exciting, intense. The best chocolate is the chocolate you like best, and the chocolate you select for cooking is the taste you get. Use a quality chocolate for quality results.

CHOCOLATE MOUSSE CAKE

When Anne Otterson cooks, something more than skill and imagination is evident—something any chocolate lover will recognize in this recipe—a passion for the delicious. Anne has studied under Jacques Pepin and Juliano Bougialli, assisted Julia Child, and delighted many of her own students and friends with masterful menus. Here she treats us to a favorite dessert for ending a meal with elegance.

**12 ounces bittersweet
  chocolate
6 ounces unsalted butter
10 eggs, separated
1½ cups sugar
1 teaspoon vanilla extract
1 tablespoon orange liqueur
  (optional)**

Preheat oven to 250 degrees. Butter and flour a nine-inch springform pan.

Break chocolate into small pieces. Melt butter in a heavy pan. Remove from heat and add chocolate, stirring vigorously until all chocolate melts. Set aside to cool.

Beat egg yolks, gradually adding one cup of the sugar. Beat for five minutes. Add cooled chocolate mixture gradually, beating on low speed. Fold in vanilla and liqueur. Set aside.

In a separate bowl, whip egg whites until soft peaks form. Add remaining sugar and beat until peaks are firm. Fold into chocolate mixture. Pour into pan and bake 2½ hours.

YIELD: 10 SERVINGS

CHOCOLATE ALMOND TORTE

⅔ cup semisweet chocolate
   chips
2 tablespoons light rum
½ cup unsalted butter,
   softened
⅔ cup sugar
3 eggs, separated
Pinch salt
2 tablespoons sugar
¼ teaspoon cream of tartar
⅓ cup pulverized almonds
¼ teaspoon almond extract
¼ teaspoon vanilla extract
¾ cup cake flour, sifted

Glaze:

6 tablespoons unsalted
   butter
½ cup semisweet chocolate
   chips
1½ teaspoons light rum

Preheat oven to 350 degrees. Butter and flour an eight-inch
cake pan.

Melt chocolate chips in a double boiler over slowly
simmering water. Remove from heat and stir in rum. In a
bowl, cream butter and sugar until fluffy. Beat in egg yolks
until well blended. In a separate bowl, beat egg whites and
salt until soft peaks form. Sprinkle in sugar and cream of
tartar and beat until peaks are stiff. Add chocolate to the
butter mixture. Stir in almonds and extracts. Immediately
stir in a fourth of the egg whites to soften batter. Add
remaining whites and flour alternating a third of each at a
time and folding until each is completely incorporated.

Pour batter into cake pan and spread to fill. Bake 25
minutes. Cake is done when puffed and a tester inserted
about three inches from edges is withdrawn clean. The
center should be soft. Remove cake from oven and allow to
cool in pan 10 minutes. Turn onto a rack to cool
thoroughly. Refrigerate before adding glaze.

To prepare glaze, melt butter and chocolate chips in a
double boiler. Remove from heat and stir in rum. Cool
thoroughly, then spread over cold cake. Refrigerate.

YIELD: 6 TO 8 SERVINGS

*For eating from the bar,
chocolate choices can suit
just about any preference.
For cooking, however, some
restrictions apply. Chocolate
is either sweetened or
unsweeted, the latter offering
few choices to the cook.
Sweetened chocolate covers a
wide range from semisweet to
very bittersweet. Milk
chocolate is not a substitute.
Avoid compound or confec-
tioner's chocolate and select
chocolate that is made from
chocolate liqueur and cocoa
butter. And if vanilla is an
ingredient, be certain it's
vanilla and not vanillin.
Store chocolate in a cool, dry
place. Chocolate with a pale
"bloom" is not spoiled. The
bloom will vanish when
heated.*

SWEDISH TORTE

A traditional family recipe often used to butter someone up. It works.

½ cup unsalted butter,
   softened
½ cup sugar
4 egg yolks
½ teaspoon vanilla extract
¼ cup milk
¾ cup sifted flour
1 teaspoon baking powder

Meringue:

Pinch salt
4 egg whites
1 cup sugar
½ teaspoon almond extract
¼ cup chopped pecans
   (or chopped blanched
   almonds)

Filling:

1 pint fresh ripe
   strawberries
1 cup heavy cream,
   whipped

Preheat oven to 325 degrees. Butter and flour two ten-inch springform pans.

Cream butter and sugar until fluffy. In a separate bowl, beat egg yolks with vanilla and continue beating while alternately adding milk, flour, and baking powder. Pour batter into baking pans. (Layers will be thin.)

Add salt to egg whites and beat until stiff. Gradually beat in sugar and almond extract. Pile half of the meringue on each layer of batter, sprinkle with nuts, and bake 45 to 50 minutes or until meringue is dry. Remove from oven and allow to cool in pans.

When ready to serve, remove one layer to a serving plate. Cover with strawberries and whipped cream. Place other layer on top, meringue side up.

YIELD: 10 SERVINGS

FRENCH APPLE CAKE

Pippins are our favorite apples for this cake. Substitute Granny Smiths if necessary. A creme fraiche or cream chantilly topping works well.

2¾ cups flour
¾ cup sugar
1 teaspoon baking powder
¼ teaspoon salt
¾ cup unsalted butter
2 eggs, beaten
2 pounds apples, peeled,
   cored, sliced
2 cups water
½ cup sugar
¼ cup fresh lemon juice

Topping:

½ cup sugar
2 teaspoons cinnamon

Preheat oven to 375 degrees. Butter a ten-inch cake pan.

Sift dry ingredients. Cut butter into small pieces and blend into flour mixture until crumbly, as if making a pastry dough. Mix in eggs and form into a ball. Press dough into sides and bottom of cake pan. Wrap with plastic and refrigerate.

Cook apples, water, sugar, and lemon juice until liquid thickens. Remove from heat and stir. Spoon apple filling into dough-lined pan. Combine sugar and cinnamon and sprinkle over top. Bake one hour or slightly longer, if necessary.

YIELD: 8 SERVINGS

To make creme chantilly: Whip one cup of heavy cream and add ½ teaspoon vanilla extract and 3 table-spoons sifted confectioner's sugar. Blend until smooth.

BLACKBERRY CAKE

½ cup unsalted butter,
    softened
1 cup sugar
2 eggs, beaten
¼ cup buttermilk
1 teaspoon baking soda
1 teaspoon cinnamon
1 teaspoon ground cloves
1 teaspoon grated nutmeg
1¾ cups flour
1 cup fresh blackberries

Icing:

½ cup unsalted butter
2 cups powdered sugar
1 egg
1 teaspoon vanilla extract

Preheat oven to 350 degrees. Butter and flour two eight-inch cake pans.

Cream butter and add sugar. Beat until fluffy. Add eggs and buttermilk, beating well. Sift together soda, spices, and flour and add in batches to butter mixture, mixing well after each addition. Fold in blackberries. Pour batter into cake pans and bake 20 to 25 minutes or until inserted tester is withdrawn clean. Do not overbake. Remove from oven to cool. Turn onto cooling racks.

Prepare icing by creaming butter until light. Add sugar gradually, and add egg and vanilla, mixing well after each addition. When cake has completely cooled, spread icing over bottom layer. Add top layer and spread remaining icing over top and sides. Garnish with blackberries, if desired.

YIELD: 10 TO 12 SERVINGS

CINNAMON PLUM CAKE

1 cup unsalted butter
1 cup packed brown sugar
2 eggs
2 teaspoons vanilla extract
3 cups sifted whole wheat
   flour
2 teaspoons baking powder
½ teaspoon baking soda
½ teaspoon cinnamon
2 cups apple juice

Almond Topping:

½ cup sliced almonds
¼ cup butter
¼ cup honey
1 tablespoon milk

Filling:

8 ounces cream cheese,
   softened
2 tablespoons powdered
   sugar
1 tablespoon plum brandy
   (or apple juice)
½ pound plums, pitted
½ cup sugar
1 cinnamon stick
1½ teaspoons cornstarch
1 tablespoon fresh lemon
   juice
1 tablespoon water

Preheat oven to 350 degrees. Butter and flour two nine-inch cake pans.

Cream butter and brown sugar. Add eggs and vanilla and beat until smooth. Sift together flour, baking powder, soda, and cinnamon. Add flour mixture to batter in batches, alternating with the apple juice and beating well after each addition. Pour into cake pans and bake 40 minutes or until inserted tester is withdrawn clean. Remove from oven to cool a few minutes before turning out onto racks.

In a small mixing bowl, beat together cream cheese, powdered sugar and brandy until fluffy. Set aside.

Chop plums into half-inch pieces. Combine with sugar in a saucepan and let stand uncovered, stirring occasionally, until sugar dissolves in juices. Add cinnamon stick and heat mixture to boiling. Reduce heat and simmer uncovered until plums are soft. Combine cornstarch, lemon juice, and water and stir into plum mixture. Cook until it thickens and bubbles for three minutes, stirring constantly. Remove cinnamon. Refrigerate uncovered until thoroughly chilled.

Preheat oven broiler. In a separate saucepan over medium heat, combine almonds, butter, honey, and milk, stirring constantly until butter melts and mixture barely bubbles, about five minutes. Remove from heat. Place one cake layer on a baking sheet and spread almond mixture over the top. Broil six inches from heat until mixture bubbles and turns golden brown. Remove from heat to cool.

Place second cake layer on serving plate and spread cream cheese mixture over the top. Spread plum mixture over cream cheese. Place almond-covered cake layer on top.

*Plums know their ABC's—
they contain those vitamins.
Over 140 kinds of plums are
grown in California.*

BANANA CAKE

¾ cup unsalted butter,
  softened
1½ cups sugar
2 eggs
1 cup mashed bananas
2 cups sifted cake flour
1 teaspoon baking powder
1 teaspoon baking soda
½ teaspoon salt
½ cup buttermilk
½ cup chopped pecans
1 cup flaked coconut

Filling:

½ cup sugar
2 tablespoons flour
½ cup whipping cream
2 tablespoons unsalted
  butter
¼ teaspoon salt
½ cup chopped pecans
1 teaspoon vanilla extract

Frosting:

½ cup unsalted butter,
  softened
1 pound powdered sugar,
  sifted
¼ cup milk
1½ teaspoons vanilla extract

Generally, when a baked dessert recipe calls for softened butter, the butter should still be slightly firm. If softened too much, the oil will separate out, preventing a fluffy mixture when butter, sugar, and eggs are combined. This fluffiness is important to the outcome of many cakes, brownies, cookies, or other baked sweets.

Preheat oven to 375 degrees. Butter and flour two nine-inch cake pans.

Cream butter and sugar until fluffy. Add eggs and beat two minutes. Add banana, beat two minutes. Sift together dry ingredients and add to batter alternately with buttermilk. Stir in nuts. Pour into cake pans and gently press coconut onto batter. Bake 30 minutes or until inserted tester is withdrawn clean. Remove from oven and cool in pans 10 minutes. Turn onto racks to cool thoroughly.

To prepare filling, combine sugar, flour, cream, and butter in a saucepan over medium heat. Stir until mixture thickens. Do not boil. Stir in salt, pecans, and vanilla. Remove from heat to cool.

Put one cake layer on a serving plate. Spread top with half the filling mixture. Place other layer on top and spread remaining filling on top.

To prepare frosting, cream butter until light and add half the sugar, beating constantly. Add milk and remaining sugar alternately until mixture achieves spreading consistency. Blend in vanilla. Frost sides of the cake and sprinkle with coconut to garnish, if desired.

YIELD: 10 TO 12 SERVINGS

ITALIAN CREAM COCONUT CAKE

1 cup unsalted butter,
  softened
2 cups sugar
5 eggs, separated
2 cups cake flour
1 teaspoon soda
1 cup buttermilk
1 teaspoon vanilla extract
1 cup sweetened coconut
1 cup chopped pecans

Frosting:

8 ounces cream cheese,
  softened
¼ cup unsalted butter,
  softened
1 pound powdered sugar
1 teaspoon vanilla
Pecan halves (garnish)

Preheat oven to 350 degrees. Butter and flour three eight-inch cake pans.

In a large mixing bowl, cream butter and sugar until fluffy. In a separate bowl, beat egg yolks and add flour and soda. Add to butter mixture alternately with buttermilk. Beat well. Add vanilla, coconut, and pecans. In a separate bowl, beat egg whites with a pinch of salt until stiff. Fold into batter. Divide batter evenly between pans and bake 30 minutes. Remove from oven and cool in pans 10 minutes. Turn onto cooling racks.

Prepare frosting by combining all ingredients and blending until smooth and creamy. When cake has completely cooled, place one layer on a serving plate and spread frosting over the top. Repeat for remaining layers, then frost around the sides. Top with pecans.

YIELD: 10 SERVINGS

Grading of eggs has nothing to do with color, freshness, or size. Eggs are graded shortly after being laid. Eggs graded AA have firm yolk membranes and a high percentage of thick white. These premium eggs are worth the price if you plan to whip whites or if you go through eggs rather slowly. Grade A eggs have weaker yolks and thinner whites. For boiling or scrambling eggs in quantity, these are fine. Store eggs in their carton in the refrigerator —not on an open rack. The shells are porous and eggs absorb odors and lose moisture easily.

APPLE CAKE

3 eggs
1 cup safflower oil
2 cups sugar
1 teaspoon vanilla extract
2 cups flour
1 teaspoon baking soda
1 teaspoon cinnamon
½ teaspoon salt
4 cups peeled and chopped apples (golden delicious preferred)

Frosting:

8 ounces cream cheese, softened
2 cups powdered sugar
Grated rind of 1 lemon
Lemon juice

Preheat oven to 350 degrees. Butter and flour a baking pan (13 x 9 inches).

Beat together eggs and oil. Gradually add sugar and vanilla. In a separate bowl, combine dry ingredients. Add to egg mixture gradually, blending in at low speed. Fold in apples. Bake 45 to 55 minutes. Remove from oven and cool thoroughly.

Blend together frosting ingredients and add enough lemon juice to make it spreadable. When cake has completely cooled in pan, spread with frosting.

YIELD: 14 TO 16 SERVINGS

BUMPY BROWNIES IN COOKIE DISGUISE

2 ounces unsweetened
  chocolate
6 ounces semisweet
  chocolate
2 tablespoons butter
¼ cup flour
¼ teaspoon baking powder
Dash of salt
2 eggs
¾ cup sugar
2 teaspoons instant coffee,
  dry
½ teaspoon vanilla extract
6 ounces semisweet
  chocolate chips
2¼ cups chopped walnuts
  or pecans

Preheat oven to 350 degrees. In a double boiler, melt first
two chocolates with butter, stirring until very smooth.

Sift together flour, baking powder, and an eighth-teaspoon
salt. Set aside. Beat eggs with sugar, coffee, and vanilla until
fluffy. Stir in chocolate mixture by hand (or on low speed
with an electric mixer), followed by flour mixture, just to
combine. Do not overmix. Stir in chocolate chips and nuts.
Drop by heaping teaspoons onto a cookie sheet—ungreased
and covered with foil. Bake 10 to 12 minutes. Surface of
brownies will be dry and shiny when done. Do not
overbake.

YIELD: 16 TO 24 BROWNIES

Index

Acorn squash ravoli, with
   marjoram, 163
Aioli sauce
   for salmon, 194
   for vegetables, 34
Albacore, Pacific, with salsa, 199
Almond(s)
   butter, 62
   California grown, 59
   chicken stir fry with, 217
   mushroom pate, 1
   removing skins from, 117
   rice pilaf and, 174
   sugared, 279
   tart, 278
   zucchini and eggplant with, 159
Amaretto freeze, 266
Apple(s)
   baked, pancake, 61
   with cabbage and walnuts, 164
   cake, 296, 301
   chicken curry with, 215
   cucumber mint salad with, 108
   pudding, 286
   and nut coffeecake, 53
   sauteed chicken with, 225
   and spinach salad, 117
   stuffing for pork, 251
   types of, for baking, 286
Applesauce muffins, 49
Artichoke hearts
   and mushrooms, baked, 166
   preparation of, 166
   in salads, 118, 121, 128, 138
Artichoke soup, cream of, 93
Asparagus
   and chicken stir fry, 215
   and lasagne, 182
   mousse, with orange sauce, 153
   salad, with lemon herb dressing,
      108
   with sesame dip, 2
   sweet and sour, 154
Avocado(s)
   and chicken breasts, 223
   and chicken curry, 215
   and crab casserole, 210
   and mushroom salad, 102
   ripeness of, 31
   and shrimp salad, 137
   soup, 81

Bacon
   and eggs with herb sauce, 67
   with grilled shrimp appetizer, 21
Banana(s)
   cake, 299
   curry salad, 110
   and orange roughy, 204
Barbecue. See Grilled meats, Grilled
      seafood.
Basil
   butter for fish, 196, 203
   as a garnish, 160
   growing and preserving, 122, 137
      203
   and infused vinegars, 115
   kinds of, 122
   pesto, 178
   sauce for shrimp appetizer, 33

Beans, dried
   salad (Basque), 104
   soup, 98, 99
Beans, green, salad, 107
Beef
   carne asada, 257
   carpaccio, 13
   fajitas, 35
   flank steak, 246
   grilled, 246, 255
   marinades for, 246, 247, 255
   mustard for, 247
   raw, as appetizer, 10, 13
   stew with salsa, 258
   stir fry with broccoli, 256
   triangle tip, 255
Bell peppers. See Peppers, sweet.
Bel Paese, and pasta, 177
Berries
   blackberries, 269, 297
   blueberries, 51, 269, 276
   cranberries, 37
   marinated, 269
   raspberries, 268, 269, 271, 279
   selecting fresh, 269
   strawberries, 45, 85, 120, 268
Blackberry cake, 297
Blintz souffle, 72
Blueberry coffeecake, 51
Blueberry pie, 276
Blue cheese, 27
   dressing, 149
   Roquefort chicken salad, 132
   Roquefort tartines, with walnuts,
      27
Bok choy, 218
Bread
   baking, 41, 42, 43
   cornsticks, 43
   crisps, herbed, 24
   French, 42
   lemon tea, 44
   Mexican corn spoon bread, 41
   rolls, French, stuffed, 75
   strawberry nut, 45
   stuffed, 74, 75, 76
   tartines, Roquefort, 27
   whole wheat pumpkin, 47
Broccoli
   and beef stir fry, 256
   and chicken salad, 131
   chicken pasta salad with, 127
   cooking, 164
   curried, soup, 91
   flan, 157
   and onions, baked, 156
   puree, 7
   sauce and pasta, 184
   and seafood quiche, 65
   souffle, 70
   soup, with cheddar cheese, 91
   vinaigrette salad, 109
Brownies, 302
Brown rice and spinach, 172
Butter
   basil, for fish, 196, 203
   flavored, for breads, 62
   for dessert baking, 299
   garlic, for scallops, 208
   mustard basil, 203
   pistachio, for grilled fish, 202
   unsalted, 62

Cabbage
   red, with chicken, 213
   with apples and walnuts, 164
Cake
   apple, 301
   banana, 299
   blackberry, 297
   chocolate mousse, 293
   cinnamon plum, 298
   coconut, Italian cream, 300
   French apple, 296
   See also Torte.
Camembert
   creamed, 9
   and pecan spread, 11
Capers, 20, 197
Caramel sauce, for fresh fruit, 268
Caraway seeds, 167
Carne asada, 257
Carpaccio, 13
Carrots, 91
   with pistachios and Cointreau,
      165
Caviar
   souffle roll, 5
   spread, 4
Ceviche, 28
Cheese
   blue-veined, 27
   Camembert, 9, 11
   Cheddar, 91, 228
   feta, 106, 125, 189
   goat, 8, 216
   Gorgonzola, 27
   Grecian flaming, 8
   Jack, 228
   mascarpone, 277
   mozzarella, 162, 181
   Parmesan, 76, 180
   and pasta, 177
   queso Chihuahua, 228
   queso fresco, 228
   ricotta, 179, 181, 214
   Romano, 178, 180
   Roquefort, 27, 132
   spread, with pecans, 11
   Stilton, 6, 27
   Swiss, 167
Cheesecake, 288, 289
   chocolate, 291
   Kahlua, 290
Cherry tomatoes, stuffed, 3
Chervil, 141
Chevre. See Goat cheese.
Chicken
   almond stir fry, 217
   baked with ginger root, 232
   and broccoli pasta salad, 127
   chilaquiles, 231
   Chinese, with asparagus, 215
   curry, with apples and avocado,
      215
   enchiladas, 228, 230
   flautas, 229
   grilled, with herb mustard, 236
   herb, with grapes in wine sauce,
      221
   marinated, and broccoli salad, 131
   mustard puree, appetizer, 14
   paillards, preparing, 224
   Peking, in tortillas, 218
   and salad greens, 130
   sesame, 219

See also Chicken breasts, Chicken
   salad.
Chicken breasts
   with chili stuffing, 234
   with crabmeat stuffing, 212
   with goat cheese, honey, and
      thyme, 216
   with grapes in wine sauce, 221
   in herb mustard, grilled 236
   and prosciutto, 214
   sauteed, with avocado, 223
   with spinach cheese stuffing, 214
   wrapped in red cabbage, 213
Chicken salad
   Chinese, 135
   Cobb variation, 111
   cucumber, spicy, 136
   layered, 134
   Roquefort, 132
   won ton, 133
Chilaquiles, chicken, 231
Chilies
   in California cooking, 171
   and salsa, 29, 31
   substituting fresh, 29
   types of, 171
Chiles rellenos, 261
Chili, 259
Chocolate
   almond tart, 294
   brownies, 302
   cheesecake, 291
   chip pie, 274
   leaves as garnish, 291
   melting, 265
   mousse cake, 293
   mousse freeze, 265
   pecan tart, 292
   types of, 292, 294
Choucroute, 252
Chutney, cranberry, 37
Cilantro, 178
   pesto, 178
   slaw, 119
Cioppino, 97
Cinnamon, 52
Cobb salad, 111
Coconut cake, 300
Coffeecakes, 50–56
Cookies
   brownies, 302
   Imperial (butter), 287
   lemon squares, frosted, 284
   peanut butter, 287
   walnut dreams, 285
Coriander, 178
Corn and barbecued vegetables, 168
Cornsticks, 43
Crab
   casserole, 210
   quiche, 66
   puffs, 25
   and red snapper, 197
   salad, 143
   stuffing for chicken breasts, 212
   stuffing for mushrooms, 22
   tacos, 36
Cranberries, 37
Cream of tartar, 281
Creme chantilly, 296
Creme fraiche, 7
   strawberries and, 268
Crepes, rosemary, with turkey and
   Gruyere, 77

Croutons, 89
Crust, dessert
   butter crunch, 273
   graham cracker, 289
   zwieback crumb, for cheesecake,
      289
Cucumber
   chicken salad, 136
   mint salad, 108
   soup, 84
Curry
   banana, salad, 110
   dip, 32
   chicken, 12, 15
   lamb, 244
Custard. See Flan.

Date(s)
   apple pudding with, 286
   baking with, 46
   cakes, 57
   California grown, 59
Dessert toppings
   caramel sauce, 268
   chocolate leaves, 291
   creme chantilly, 296
   creme fraiche, 268
   raspberries, 271
Dill
   butter, for seafood, 196
   and champagne sauce, for salmon,
      194
   and peas, 155
   and zucchini soup, 86
Dressings, salad, 121, 146–149.
   See also Vinaigrettes.
Duckling, in orange sauce, 222

Eggplant, 158, 159
   Oriental, 253
Eggs
   baked, with bacon and herb
      sauce, 67
   grading of, 300
   hard-cooked, 67
   and mushrooms, 68
   See also Quiche, Souffle, Flan.
Enchiladas, chicken, 228, 230
Endive, Belgian, 7
   and mushroom salad, 103
   Roquefort chicken salad and, 132
Epazote, 98

Fajitas, chicken, 35
Fennel salad, 112
Feta cheese, 106, 189
   and angel hair pasta, 189
   with pasta salad and spinach, 125
   tomatoes with dill and, 106
Fettuccine, 183
   salad with roasted peppers and
      shrimp, 123
   with smoked salmon sauce, 185
   spinach, and fish in aioli sauce,
      194
   vegetable, carbonara, 186
Fish
   and ceviche, 28
   freshness of, 197, 198
   soup, 94

   stew, 92
   See also Seafood, and specific
      varieties of fish.
Flan, 280
   broccoli, 157
Flat-leaf (Italian) parsley, 86
Flautas, chicken, 229
Fontina cheese, and pasta, 177
Freeze
   Amaretto, 266
   chocolate mousse, 265
   kiwi ice, 267
French toast, Mexican, 63
Fruit, dried, 59
Fruit, fresh
   California grown, 283
   as desserts, 267–269, 283
   dipped in caramel sauce, 268
   exotic varieties, 283
   salad, with marinated pork, 145
   in soup, 85
   See also Apples, Berries, and
      individual varieties.

Garlic
   beurre rouge, 211
   butter, for scallops, 208
   dressing, 147
   sauce, for grilled fish, 211
   storage of, 33, 137
Gazpacho, 83
Ginger root, 17, 219
   with baked chicken, 232
Gnocchi, spinach, 179
Goat cheese, 8, 216
Gorgonzola, 27, 177
Grand Marnier, 277
Grape(s)
   chicken in wine sauce with, 221
   sauce for poultry, 237
Grilled meats, 227
   barbecue sauce for, 248, 255
   carne asada, 257
   chicken, 35, 236
   fajitas, 35
   flank steak, marinated, 246
   lamb, 243
   marinade for, 246–249
   mustard for, 236, 247
   pork skewers, 17
   Spanish sauce for, 71
   spareribs, 255
   steak, marinated, 255
   tarragon mayonnaise for, 249
   turkey, mesquite, 235
Grilled seafood, 227
   and butter toppings, 196
   with garlic beurre rouge, 211
   halibut, 200
   kebabs, 193
   red snapper, 197
   shrimp, 21
   yellowtail, 202
Grilled vegetables, 168, 227
Guacamole, 31

Halibut, 200
Herb(s)
   butters, 196
   and chicken breasts, 221
   mayonnaise for grilled seafood, 202

mustard for grilled chicken, 236
and rice, 173
substituting fresh, 24
See also individual herbs.
Honey-fruit butter, 62

Ice cream
Amaretto freeze, 266
chocolate mousse freeze, 271
cooked, 272
desserts, 270-273
peach, 270
pie, 273
shake, Irish coffee, 270
Ice, kiwi, 267
Irish coffee shake, 270

Jack cheese, in Mexican cooking, 228
Jalapenos, 29
stuffing for chicken breasts, 225
See also Peppers, hot.
Jicama, 139

Kebabs
pork satay, 16
pork skewers, 17
seafood, 193
King salmon, 195
Kiwi, 267

Lamb
butterfly of, grilled, 243
chops, grilled, 243
curry, 244
medallions, with horseradish and cucumber, 245
noisettes of, with Pernod sauce, 242
stew, with rosemary, 241
Lasagne
Lingurian, 180
noodles, 182
spinach, 181
with smoked ham and asparagus, 182
Leeks, 84
Lemon(s), 44
rice, 176
squares, frosted, 284
souffle, chilled, 281
tea bread, 44
Lentil soup, 99
Lettuce, types of, 111, 142
Linguine
and Rock Cornish hens, 220
with spring vegetables, 188
Liqueur(s)
Amaretto, 266
Cointreau, 165
Grand Marnier, 277
for dessert making, 277
Kahlua, in cheesecake, 290
orange, 277

Marjoram, with acorn squash ravioli, 163
Marinara sauce, 183

Marinades
for grilled meats, 247–249, 255
for vegetables, 105, 154, 155
Marmalade butter, 62
Marmite, 255
Marzipan, and raspberry tart, 279
Mascarpone, orange cream, 277
Mayonnaise
baked chicken with, 232
homemade, 134
sweet pepper, for swordfish, 200
tarragon, for marinated beef, 249
Mesquite grilled turkey, 235
Mexican (and Mexican-style) dishes
burritos, shrimp and vegetable, 206
carne asada, 257
chilaquiles, 231
chiles rellenos, Guadalajara, 261
and cilantro, 178
cilantro slaw, 119
fajitas, chicken, 35
flautas, chicken, 229
French toast, 63
guacamole, 31
jalapeno stuffed chicken, 225
lentil soup, 99
salsa, 29, 31, 35
seafood, 199, 200
sopa de frijoles, 98
spoon bread, 41
tacos, crab, 36
tomatillo sauce, 231
tortilla soup, 96
Mexican vanilla, 63
Mint, and cucumber salad, 108
Mousse
asparagus, 153
raspberry, 268
shrimp and crab, 23
Mousse cake, chocolate, 265
Mozzarella
with baked zucchini, 162
and lasagne, 181
Muffins
applesauce, 49
orange almond, 46
sweet potato, 48
Mushroom(s)
almond pate, 1
and artichoke hearts, baked, 166
and artichoke soup, 93
and avocado salad, 102
Benedict, 69
bisque, 90
crab stuffed, 22
and eggs, 68
and endive salad, 103
marinated, 105
and rice, baked, 173
salad, marinated, 105
Mustard
for beef, grilled, 247
for chicken, grilled, 236

Noodles. *See* Pasta.
Nuts
almonds, 59, 174, 278, 279
California grown, 59
desserts and, 286
and dried fruits, 59
pecans, 11, 175, 286, 292
pine nuts, 169, 183
pistachios, 165

storage of, 6
walnuts, 6, 59, 164, 176, 285
Nutmeg, 55

Oatcake
with caramel nut topping, 56
frosted, 55
Oils
olive, 148
peanut, 154
safflower, 116
salad, 115
Olive oil, 148
Olives, 127
Onions, 156, 158
green, 25
pearl, 156
rings, 26
soup, 88
storage of, 26
Orange liqueurs, 277
Orange roughy, 204
Oranges, 283
Oregano, 230
Oriental (and Oriental-style) dishes
almond chicken stir fry, 217
Chinese chicken with asparagus, 217
hot and sour zucchini, 161
linguine with vegetables stir fry, 188
Peking chicken in tortillas, 218
sesame broccoli, 155
Oyster stew, 95

Pancakes, 57, 60–61
Papaya, flaming, 290
Parmesan cheese, 76
and baked sole, 203
and pasta, 177, 179, 182–187
and pesto, 178
Parsley, 126
Italian, 86
Pasta, 177–189
acorn squash ravioli, 163
angel hair, 189
with broccoli sauce, 184
fettuccine, with smoked salmon sauce, 185
with four cheeses, 177
gnocchi, 179
homemade, 177
kinds of, 183
lasagne, 180–182
linguine, with vegetables, 188
primavera, 183
spaghettini, 187
Pasta salads, 122–128
Pasta sauces
broccoli, 184
cilantro pesto, 178
marinara, 183
pesto, 178
smoked salmon, 185
Pate, mushroom and almond, 1
Pea(s), 82, 155
dilled, 155
soup, chilled, 82
Peach
ice cream, 270
pie, 275
Pecan(s)

apple pudding with, 286
cheese spread, 11
chocolate tart, 292
and herb rice, baked, 175
Pepper, 107
white, 254
Peppercorns
green, 197
Szechuan, 254
Peppers, hot, 171
jalapenos, 29, 225
poblanos, 29
serranos, 29
Peppers, sweet, 34, 123, 200
mayonnaise, for swordfish, 200
roasted, 123, 126
stuffed, 253
Pesto, 178
cilantro, 178
for pizza, 260
Lingurian lasagne with, 180
vegetable soup with, 101
zucchini with, 160
Pflaumenkuchen, 54
Pie
blueberry, 276
chocolate chip, 274
ice cream, 273
peach, 275
Pineapple, with shrimp and dill, 20
Pine nuts
and pasta, 183, 184
and rice, 169
Pizza, with chevre and pesto, 260
Plum
cake, 298
tart, 54
Poppy seed coffeecake, 50
Pork
and apple cider, 250
roast, stuffed, 251
satay (Thai), 16
skewers, marinated, 17
spareribs, barbecued, 255
stir fry, 254
Potatoes
caraway with Swiss cheese, 167
sweet, 48
Prosciutto, and chicken breasts, 214
Pumpkin bread, 47
Pumpkin seeds (pepitas), and pesto,
178

Quiche
crab, 66
seafood and broccoli, 65
spinach, 64

Radicchio, and chicken appetizer,
15
Radish salad, 113
Raisin(s)
in baking, 46
and nut butter, 62
Raspberries
marinated, 269
marzipan tart, 279
mousse, 268
selecting, 269
topping for ice cream, 271
Ratatouille nicoise, 158
Red cabbage, and chicken breasts, 213

Red snapper
in ceviche, 28
with lemon caper butter, 197
in lemon herb sauce, 198
in sherry sauce, 197
Remoulade dressing, 20, 140
Rice, 169–176
additions to, 174
brown, 172
converted, 175
herbed, 173, 175
Indian rice, 175
Japanese rice, 175
lemon, 176
long-grain, 173, 175, 176
with mushrooms, baked, 173
pilaf, 174
salad, with corn and roasted
peppers, 126
wild, 176
Ricotta cheese
in lasagne, 181
and spinach gnocchi, 179
stuffing for chicken, 214
Risotto, 169
Rock Cornish hens, 220
Rolls, stuffed French, 75
Roquefort cheese, 27
and walnut tartines, 27
and chicken salad, 132
Rosemary, 241
crepes, with turkey and gruyere, 77
lamb stew with, 241

Sabayon sauce for sea bass, 201
Safflower oil, 116
Saffron, 169
Salad dressings, 146–149. See also
Vinaigrettes.
Salads, 102–145
Salmon
in aioli sauce, 194
kinds of, 195
in peppercorn sorrel sauce, 195
poached, in champagne dill sauce,
194
smoked, in pasta salad, 124
smoked, sauce for fettuccine, 185
Salsa, 29, 31, 35
with Pacific albacore, 199
Sandwiches, 74, 76
Sauces
aioli, 34, 194
barbecue, 248
champagne dill, 194
dill or seafood, 204
garlic beurre rouge, 211
grape, for poultry, 237
herb, for bacon and eggs, 67
herb butter, 224
lemon herb, for red snapper, 198
mustard, 32
remoulade, 20
sorrel, 195
Spanish, 71
wine with grapes, 221
Sauerkraut
in choucroute, 252
Sausage, stuffed Italian, 253
Scallions, 25
Scallops, bay
in garlic butter, 208

in seafood kebabs, 193
Sea bass, 196
braised in apple cider tarragon, 201
with fresh basil butter, 196
Seafood
appetizers, 20, 23, 25, 28
and broccoli quiche, 65
basil butter for, 196, 203
caper butter for, 197
ceviche, 28
curries, 207
entrees, 193-211
kebabs, 193
mustards and, 202, 203
salads, 137–145
sauces for, 194, 195, 197, 198,
199, 204, 205
soups, 94
stew, 92, 95, 209
zarzuela, 209
See also Crab, Fish, Grilled
Seafood, Scallops, Shrimp.
Serranos, 29. See also Peppers, hot.
Sesame seed(s)
broccoli, 155
chicken, marinated, 219
dip, for asparagus, 2
Shallots, 207
storage of, 137
in vinaigrette, 129
Shrimp
with angel hair pasta and feta
cheese, 189
and artichoke salad, 138
and avocado salad, 137
cooking of, 138
and crab curry, baked, 207
and crab mousse, 23
in dill sauce, 204
dip, 30
eggplant and feta cheese salad
with, 207
and fettuccine salad, 123
grilled with bacon, 21
in kebabs, 193
with pineapple and dill, 20
and red snapper, 197
salad, molded, 142
selecting fresh, 205
spicy, in tomato herb sauce, 205
with sun-dried tomatoes, 207
and vegetable burritos, 206
and vegetable salad, 141
in wine and basil sauce, 33
Slaw, cilantro, 119
Thai, spicy, 116
Souffle
blintzes, 72
broccoli, 70
chili and cheese, 73
lemon, 281
Soups, 81–101
Sour cream coffeecake, 52
Spareribs, barbecued, 255
Spinach
with brown rice, 172
and cheese stuffing, for chicken,
214
and chicken pasta salad, 125
garnish, 128
gnocchi, 179
lasagne, 181

pasta salad with feta cheese, 126
quiche, 64
and Rock Cornish hens, 220
salad, with bacon and apple, 117
and strawberry salad, 120
Spoon bread, Mexican, 41
Sole, baked, 203
Sorrel sauce, for salmon, 195
Sour cream coffeecake, 52
Spaghettini primavera, 187
Spanish-style dishes
gazpacho, 83
sauce, for meats and eggs, 71
zarzuela, 209
Steak
marinated flank, 246
triangle tip, 255
See also Beef.
Stew
beef, 258
chili, 259
fish, 92
lamb, 241
oyster, 95
Stir fry, 215, 217
almond chicken, 217
beef, 256
hot and sour zucchini, 161
zucchini with pesto, 160
Strawberries, 85
and creme fraiche, 268
in nut bread, 45
and spinach salad, 120
soup with, 85
storage of, 45
Sweet potato muffins, 48
Sun-dried tomatoes, 180, 207
Swiss cheese with caraway potatoes, 167
Swordfish, broiled, 200

Tacos, crabmeat, 36
Tarragon
and apple cider, for sea bass, 201
butter, for seafood, 196
mayonnaise, for beef, 249
Tart
almond, 278
chocolate pecan, 292
plum, 54
raspberry marzipan, 279
Tea breads, 44–45
Thresher shark, 203
Thyme, 212
and honey sauce for chicken, 216
and zucchini soup, 87
Tomatillos, 231
Tomatoes, 94, 158, 187
cherry, 3
with dill and feta cheese, 106
in pasta salad, 122
peeling, 189
plum (Italian), 187
sauce, for stuffed chicken, 234
soup, 83, 89
sun-dried, 180, 207
Toppings. *See* Dessert toppings.
Torte
chocolate almond, 294
Swedish, 295
Tortilla(s), 229

chilaquiles, 231
soup, 96
Tuna, sandwich nicoise, 76. *See also*
Albacore, Pacific.
Turkey
crepes with Gruyere, 77
mesquite grilled, 235
smoked, salad, 129

Vanilla, 63
Veal
breast, stuffed, 238
chops, in red chili, 239
scallops, sherried, 240
Vegetable(s)
with aioli sauce, 34
cooking, 153, 154, 155, 164
dishes, 153–168
fettuccine, carbonara, 186
flan (broccoli), 157
gazpacho, 83
grilled, 168, 227
mousse (asparagus), 153
and pasta, 183, 186, 188
puree, 7
ratatouille, 158
salad, 109
and shrimp salad, 141
soup, with pesto, 101
See also individual varieties.
Vinaigrettes, 103, 109, 111, 112, 129, 131, 139, 141, 143
Balsamic, 147, 148
creamy, 146
mustard, 146
oils for, 115
and vinegars, infused, 115
Vinegars, 115, 121

Walnut(s)
cabbage and apples with, 164
California grown, 59
Chinese chicken salad with, 135
dessert bars, 285
and Stilton torta, 6
wild rice and, 176
Watercress, 129
and pea soup, 82
Wine
California, 19
in soup, 88
vinegars, 115, 121
Won tons
chicken salad with, 133
for acorn squash ravioli, 163

Yellowtail, grilled, 202

Zarzuela, 209
Zest, citrus, 13
Zucchini
baked with mozzarella, 162
and eggplant almondine, 159
hot and sour, 161
with pesto, 160
in ratatouille, 158
soup, 86, 87